Japanese

Business Glossary

by Mitsubishi Corporation

日・本・人・語

〈和英対訳〉

東洋経済新報社

Simplified Pronunciation Guide

In order to pronounce correctly the Japanese words listed in this glossary, all you need to do is learn the pronunciation of five vowels. The Japanese syllabary, which corresponds to the English alphabet, represents far fewer sounds than the letters of the alphabet. The syllabary contains only five vowels, 13 "semi-consonants" and one consonant — in all, seven less than the letters in the English language. (For the purposes of this simplified guide, we call the syllabary symbols which start with a consonant sound but end with a vowel sound "semi-consonants".)

The table on the next page renders the Japanese syllabary in alphabetical letters. It also gives the diphthongs. The vowels and consonants are always pronounced in the same way without exception.

The constant pronunciations of the vowels are:

"a" as in **a**nnounce   "e" as in p**e**n
"i " as in **i**nk   "o" as in **o**il
"u" as in p**u**t

The vowels which appear in the syllabary as part of the semi-consonants are always pronounced as shown above.

There are cases in which the vowel sound is prolonged. In such cases, in this book they are indicated with a wave-mark above the vowel: ã, ĩ, ũ, ẽ, õ.

A guide for pronouncing the consonant sounds is not necessary because when, say, "k" is coupled with the constant sound of any of the five vowels, it can have only one possible sound. The only consonant that needs an explanation is "g". This is always hard as in the English word **go**.

The diphthongs are combinations of some of the semi-consonants with the "y" line semi-consonants ending in "a" or "u" or "o". In this case, the vowel sound of the prefixed semi-consonant is eliminated.

With one exception, all Japanese words expressed in the English alphabet end with a vowel. The exception is "n". This is pronounced in a nasal way in much the same way as the English "......ng", but without sounding the "g". This consonant comes only at the end of a syllable, and therefore in the words in this glossary, it is always followed by a semi-consonant: **banzai**, **hanko**, **denshin**, etc.

Sometimes, you will find double consonants in the middle of a word, such as **chotto** and **ippai**. In this case, the preceding vowel is pronounced with a slightly rising inflection and the first of the double consonants is choked.

When two vowels come together, pronounce each separately; do not run them together: **shain** = sha·in; **teate** = te·ate.

Japanese Syllabary Expressed in Alphabetical Letters

Vowels		a	i	u	e	o
Semi-Consonants						
"k"	line	ka	ki	ku	ke	ko
"s"	line	sa	shi	su	se	so
"t"	line	ta	chi	tsu	te	to
"n"	line	na	ni	nu	ne	no
"h"	line	ha	hi	fu	he	ho
"m"	line	ma	mi	mu	me	mo
"y"	line	ya	i	yu	e	yo
"r"	line	ra	ri	ru	re	ro
"w"	line	wa	i	u	e	wo
"g"	line	ga	gi	gu	ge	go
"z"	line	za	ji	zu	ze	zo
"d"	line	da	ji	zu	de	do
"b"	line	ba	bi	bu	be	bo
"p"	line	pa	pi	pu	pe	po

Consonant

The one consonant is "n" which comes only at the end of a syllable.

Diphthongs

kya	—	kyu	—	kyo
sha	—	shu	—	sho
cha	—	chu	—	cho
nya	—	nyu	—	nyo
hya	—	hyu	—	hyo
mya	—	myu	—	myo
rya	—	ryu	—	ryo
gya	—	gyu	—	gyo
ja	—	ju	—	jo
bya	—	byu	—	byo
pya	—	pyu	—	pyo

Foreword

The Greek *logos*, meaning word, is also used to signify cosmic reason, essence, rule, etc. The thoughts and actions of a people were expressed in words and, it could be said, words in their turn moulded patterns of thinking and behavior. Truly, words constitute culture and reflect a people's history, manners and customs.

For the past eight years or so, the English-language *Tokyo Newsletter,* published every month by Mitsubishi Corporation, has been attempting to explain some typical Japanese expressions in its "Business Glossary" column. The column introduced unique Japanese business practices and expressions in a light but informative form. In order to compile this volume, more than 40 items were added to those which were first published in *Tokyo Newsletter.*

In selecting the expressions, old Japanese proverbs and ancient Chinese expressions (such as **bokushu**, meaning inflexibility or running against the current of the times to stick to old ways) have been avoided. Also left out were frequently used business expressions which could be rendered simply in English as one word (such as **ôte**, meaning checkmate). The expressions selected were those which figure in the daily conversation of Japanese businessmen and which they understand instantly

序　文

　「ことば」を意味するギリシア語の「ロゴス」はまた，理性，本質，法則などの意に用いられることは，広く知られているとおりだが，民族の思考と行動はことばとなり，逆にことばは思考と行動のパターンを形づくるともいえる。まさにことばは文化であり，民族の歴史と習俗の現われである。

　「"根まわし"を外人にどう説明したらよいだろう」「"腹芸"なんてあまりにも日本人的な感覚だから，外人にはとうていわかるまい」。

　三菱商事株式会社が発行する英文広報誌 *TOKYO NEWSLETTER*（月刊　15,000部）に，軽い話題の提供を兼ねて，日本人独特のビジネス慣習やいいまわしを紹介する短文のコラム "Business Glossary" をもうけて，8年ほどになる。その間つくり貯めたことばにさらに40語ほどを加えて上梓することとなった。

　ことばを選ぶにあたっては，日本古来のことわざや，中国からの故事名句（たとえば "墨守"）などは除外するようにした。また，ビジネス用語としても良く使われるが，英語一語で簡単に訳せるようなことば（たとえば "王手" = checkmate）は拾っていない。あくまでも日本人ビジネスマン同士で日常口にし，話題にし，おたがいすぐに通じあうが，外人には少々説明を要する，ないし誤解されるおそれのあることば，との基準で作業を進めてきたが，その結果，選んだことばに恣意的な片寄りもあるかも知れず，決して網羅的ではないこと，また短文のために，説明不足になったり一面的な解説になるなど，至らない点は多々ある

5

but which might create misunderstanding among people of other countries unless some supplementary explanation is given. Therefore, the selections are in no way intended to constitute a comprehensive glossary.

At the same time, it means that almost all of the expressions need no explanations for the Japanese reader. Moreover, the bulk of the explanations were written originally in English (by Kazuma Uyeno of Century Eibun Henshusha, Ltd.), and were translated into Japanese for the purposes of this volume. Because things which are absolutely unnecessary as explanation for Japanese have been left out, the reader is forewarned that the translation is not necessarily faithful to the original. However, some of the newly added items were first written in Japanese and translated into English as faithfully as possible.

The editor would feel amply rewarded if this small volume should provide topics for conversation between Japanese readers and their foreign friends and help smooth the way for better international communication.

Shigeo Momoki
General Manager
Corporate Communications Office

こと，あらかじめお断わりしておきたい。

　反面，日本人には不必要な説明語が大半を占めるわけだが，この語集はもともと英文で書き起こされ（センチュリー英文編集社・上野一磨氏），このほど初めて和文訳をつくったもので，和訳にあたっては，日本人にはまったく説明不要な事柄は省いている。したがって，厳密な対訳にはなっていないこと，ご承知おきいただきたい。

　この本が，読者と，読者の外国友人との話題の種となり，おたがいのコミュニケーションの潤滑剤となるならば，編者の大いに喜びとするところである。

　なお，ローマ字は，ヘボン式によった。

編　者

Abura wo uru

"What is he doing? " "He's selling oil." This is a respectable activity, but if the answer were translated directly into simple Japanese, it can take on a derogatory meaning describing the way a person applies himself to his job. This is because **abura wo uru** has another meaning beside "to sell oil". The other meaning is "to loaf on the job"

In the days before electricity, street vendors went around town selling rapeseed oil for use in lanterns. As they didn't seem to be applying themselves very assiduously to their work, the term **abura wo uru** was born which nowadays is frequently used to describe a businessman who slips out of the office to pass time away in a coffee shop.

Aisatsu-mawari

After the week-long year-end and New Year holidays, government offices and commercial houses reopen for business on January 4 or 5. But the foreign businessman who visits a Japanese company on that day expecting to conduct business is often frustrated.

油を売る

"What is he doing？""He's selling oil"この会話の答え selling oil は立派な商売であるが,これを日本語にそのまま訳すと,ある人の仕事ぶりをそしるような意味をもつ。「油を売る」には to sell oil とは別に, loaf on the job（仕事をさぼる）の意味があるからだ。

電気がまだ発明されていなかったころ,行商人は "あんどん" 用の油を,通りから通りへ呼び売りして歩いたものである。彼等は仕事に精を出しているようにはみえなかった。ここから「油を売る」といえば,現在では会社を抜け出して喫茶店で時間をつぶしているサラリーマンを指すようになった。

挨拶まわり

年末年始の1週間の休みが終わると,官庁や会社では,1月の4日か5日あたりから,仕事始めになる。ところが外国人がこの日に仕事をしようと思って日本の会社を訪問すると,とまどうことがよくある。

Offices reopen, but the main business of the day is **aisatsu-mawari** after the employees have listened to the president's traditional New Year speech in which he outlines his plans and expectations for the new year and exhorts the staff to greater endeavors. **Aisatsu-mawari** is "making a round of courtesy calls". The employees make calls not only on people in other departments of the same company but also on outside clients to say, "Happy New Year! Please continue to favor us this year again".

The term is not limited to New Year's courtesy calls. The courtesy calls which an executive makes when he takes up a new post in Japan are also **aisatsu-mawari**.

→ Gashi-kõkan

Aka-chõchin

Many Japanese corporate workers make it a habit to drop in at an **aka-chõchin** before they head for home after a day's work. **Aka** means red and **chõchin** lantern, but don't jump to the conclusion that the phrase means a "red light" establishment.

This huge lantern, about a meter in diameter and made of paper pasted over bamboo ribbing is prominently displayed in front of typically Japanese drinking establishments. It is an indication that the shop serves **sake** and simple popular

オフィスは開いているのだが，この日の主な仕事は，まず社長恒例の年頭の辞，新年の抱負と期待，社員への激励の言葉を拝聴する。それからが「挨拶まわり」（making a round of courtesy calls）である。社内のほかの部課の人たちばかりでなく，外のお得意先にも行って「あけましておめでとうございます。今年もよろしくお願いします」（Happy New year！ Please continue to favor us this year again.）と挨拶する。

「挨拶まわり」は新年だけとは限らない。転任の役職員が着任して表敬訪問するのも，やはり「挨拶まわり」である。

→ 賀詞交換

赤ちょうちん

日本のサラリーマンは，1日の仕事を終えて家路につく前に，「赤ちょうちん」へよく寄る。「赤」は red，「ちょうちん」は lantern だが，早とちりして red light（赤線区域）のことだ，などと思ってはいけない。

この大ちょうちんは，竹ひごの骨組みに紙を貼った，直径1メートルほどのもの。日本式の一杯のみ屋の入口に，それとはっきり分かるようにぶらさげてある。「赤ちょうちん」は，「この店では，酒とちょっとしたおつまみ程度のものをお出しします。お値段は安く，気楽な仲間同士の雰囲気で楽しめます」という目印である。2時間ほど時を過ご

dishes, that its prices are cheap and that an informal camaraderie prevails. A person can enjoy himself for a couple of hours at a cost of less than $10. The **aka-chōchin** may be considered the Japanese counterpart of the English pub.

In addition to the red lantern, there hangs above the doorway a **nawa-norén**, a short curtain with the shop's name on it. Thus, both **aka-chō-chin** and **nawa-noren** can be used to mean an inexpensive drinking place.

→ **Noren, Chotto ippai**

Ama-kudari

Ama-kudari is written with the Chinese ideograms which mean "to descend from heaven". The character for **ama** (heaven) stands for the emperor, shogun, or the central government. The expression is used to mean the taking of a top post in a private company by a person who has retired from high government office.

Ama-kudari is also used to refer to a person coming from a different division in a government ministry or business corporation to become the head of another division or section, or to a manager in a parent company being appointed president of a subsidiary.

In Japan, personnel shifts between companies are rare and the manager of a department in a

しても，1人あたり10ドルとかからない。赤ちょうちんは，イギリスのパブの日本版と思えばいい。

　赤ちょうちんのほかに，入口にはしゅろで編んだなわで作った短いカーテン「縄のれん」がかかっている。「縄のれん」と「赤ちょうちん」はともに大衆酒場の意味につかわれる。

　→のれん，ちょっと一杯

天下り

　字義は「天」（Ama）より降りること。天には天皇，将軍，中央政府などの長の意味がある。このことから，中央政府の高官などが定年後民間企業などの主要ポストにつくことを意味するようになった。また，他の部局から自分たちの部局の長が任命されたり，子会社の社長に親会社の部長などが任命されたりするときなどにも「天下り」といわれる。

　企業間人事異動がきわめてまれであり，部門の長はその部門の「生え抜き」で占められることが通常であるから，

big corporation is almost invariably promoted from among the staff of that department. Consequently, an **ama-kudari** appointment has a somewhat unpleasant ring to the staff of a department which gets a manager from the outside.

In Japan of the Middle Ages, the word **ame no shita** (literally, under the heaven) meant not just all Japan but the entire world. Another way of pronouncing the ideogram for **ame no shita** is **tenka,** and even today, election as the prime minister of Japan or an exceptional rise to a top position is referred to as **tenka wo toru** (to take or seize power).

→ **Chūto-saiyo, Sekigahara, Tozama**

Aota-gai

Aota-gai is a phrase which originally was used in agriculture. Today, it is scarcely used in the farming communities but has become an indispensable part of the industrial vocabulary.

In the old days, it meant "buying rice on the stalk" before it was harvested. It is similar to buying beef on the hoof or wool on the sheep's back. Poor farmers in need of cash received money from merchants in exchange for a promise to deliver the rice when it was harvested.

Aota-gai (literally, to buy a green paddy field) is used today to describe the act of companies "raiding" schools to "sign up" students who are

「天下り人事」は「生え抜き」でない人が長になる点，迎える側にとって多少愉快でない響きが含まれる。

　なお，天下（Ame-no-shita ＝ Tenka）は，中世日本人にとって全日本というより全世界を意味した。現代でも「天下をとる」は，異例の出世をしたとか，日本の首相になるとかのときにつかわれる。

　→中途採用，関が原，外様

青田買い

　「青田買い」は，もともと農業用語であった。今日では，農業用語としてつかわれるのはごくまれで，企業社会に欠かせない用語のひとつになっている。昔は，刈入れまえに buying rice on the stalk の意味だった。牛肉を生きた牛のまま買い予約するとか，羊毛を羊から刈るまえに買い予約するのと同じである。貧しい農家が，現金をどうしても必要なとき，穫れたお米で返す約束で，商人から前借りすることである。

　「青田買い」（直訳すると，to buy a green paddy field）は，企業が学校にアタックをかけて，翌春卒業見込みの学

scheduled to graduate in the spring of the following year. Sometimes, instead of **aota-gai**, people
use **aota-gari** (to harvest the green paddy) to describe the intensity with which companies conduct their premature recruiting.

→ **Shin·nyū-shain**

Apointo

The Japanese lexicon is full of words borrowed
from foreign languages and altered somewhat in
form and sometimes even in meaning to make
them fit into Japanese life. **Apointo** is a corruption of "appointment".

Although it is used in the standard sense to
mean a prearranged meeting, it is not uncommon
for a visitor with an **apointo** to be kept waiting
because someone got there before him, quite
often a person who dropped in without an appointment. The fact that a person "just happen-
ed to be in the neighborhood" is sufficient reason
to gain entry because a Japanese executive or a
knowledgeable foreign businessman in Japan rarely refuses to see someone who drops in without
an **apointo**.

In all fairness, however, it must be said that the

生から入社の約束をとりつけることをいう。「青田買い」のかわりに「青田刈り」（to reap the green paddy field）ということもある。企業が，新入社員の獲得に早いうちから一所懸命に奔走するさまをいう。

　→ 新入社員

アポイント

　日本語には，外国語からの借り物で，日本の生活に合うよう，語形とか，ときには意味まで変えて使っている言葉が，たくさんある。「アポイント」は，appointment が略されたものである。

　ふつうは，面会の日時をあらかじめ取り決めておくことの意味につかう。しかしアポイントがあって訪問しても，待たされることはざらにある。前の訪問者がまだ中にいるとか，アポイントなしで訪ねた人がいることが，しょっちゅうである。「ちょっと近所まできましたので」というのが，突然訪ねるばあいの立派な理由になるからだ。日本人も日本に明るい外国のビジネスマンも，アポイントなしでやって来たからといって面会を拒まれることはめったにない。

younger breed of international-minded Japanese businessman is more scrupulous about strictly keeping appointments.

Arubaito

Arubaito is not a native Japanese word, but the Japanized form of the German word "arbeit", meaning work. As in the case of thousands of foreign words which the Japanese have adopted, the original meaning has been changed to suit Japanese purposes.

Thus **arubaito** refers to part-time work or temporary work or moonlighting. Students who work to earn pocket money or to pay tuition are doing **arubaito**.

Companies often carry a category of workers called **arubaito** who work regular, full hours but are treated differently from regular employees. They are paid by the hour or by the day and are not given any of the substantial fringe benefits of regular employees. Piecework **arubaito** is usually done at home.

→ **Naishoku**

Banzai

Do not be frightened when you hear a group of Japanese shouting **banzai** in an airport lobby. It is not the **banzai** attack cry heard in World War II movies, rather they are sending off one of their

しかし，全体としてみると，若い世代の日本のビジネスマンは，国際感覚を身につけるようになり，アポイントメントを時間どおり，きちんと守るようになってきた。

アルバイト

「アルバイト」は，もともと日本語ではない。ドイツ語のArbeit（労働の意）が日本語化した言葉である。本来の意味から変わって日本的なものになっている外国語は何千とある。

このように「アルバイト」は，パートタイムや一時的な仕事などのことをいう。小遣いや学資をかせぐため，学生は「アルバイト」をする。

会社もアルバイトと称する部類の人を雇うことがよくある。正規の時間どおり働いても，正社員と待遇の違う人達である。賃金は時給ないし日給で，正社員と違って賃金外の諸手当は支給されない。出来高払い制のアルバイトは，家ですることが多い。

→ 内職

ばんざい

一団の日本人が空港ロビーで「ばんざい」を唱和したからといって，驚いてはいけない。第2次大戦の戦争映画に出てくる "バンザイ特攻" ではない。海外に赴任する同僚

colleagues leaving for an overseas post.

Banzai is literally "ten thousand years". On the Emperor's Birthday, thousands of people gather in the courtyard of the Imperial Palace to chant **banzai**, in which case it means "Long Live the Emperor".

Banzai is also a simple "hurray" for felicitous occasions. Winning a baseball game, completing a building, getting elected to office or finding the right word for a crossword puzzle calls for a **banzai**. Surrounded by friends and relatives at a railway station, newlyweds are sent off on their honeymoon with a rather embarrassing attention-attracting **banzai**.

Batsu

Batsu is an important institution in Japanese society. Knowing what **batsu** a certain person belongs to helps greatly in constructing your human relations in the society. In general terms, **batsu** means clique, faction or clan.

There are various types of **batsu**. Major Japanese political parties often have factions (**ha-batsu**) which are like parties within the party. Each faction is constituted around an influential politician and is usually known by his name.

The **kei-batsu** is not necessarily an organized group as such, but it speaks with a loud voice. It can be called the clan whose members are

の見送りにきているのである。

「ばんざい」を直訳すると "ten thousand years" となる。天皇誕生日に幾千もの人が皇居の庭に参集して「ばんざい」を繰り返す。このときの「ばんざい」は "Long Live the Emperor" である。

おめでたいときの「ばんざい」は "hurrah" と同じだ。野球の試合に勝ったとき，ビルが竣工したとき，クロスワード・パズルでぴったりの単語を思いついたとき，「ばんざい」である。駅のホームで友人・親戚に囲まれて，ほやほやのカップルが新婚旅行に出かけるときも，「ばんざい」で送られる。これは，人目についてきまりの悪い「ばんざい」かもしれない。

閥 (ばつ)

「閥」は，日本社会の重要な仕組みである。その人がどの「閥」に属しているかを知っておくと，日本の社会で人間関係を良くするのに役立つ。一般に「閥」とは faction, clique ないし clan である。閥にもいろいろある。政党には「派閥」(faction) があり，党内党 (parties within the party) のようなものである。派閥は勢力ある政治家を中心にした集まりで，その人の名を冠するのが普通である。

「閨閥」は，必ずしも「閥」として組織だったものではないが，やはり大きな影響力をもつ一族といってよい。血縁や姻戚関係 (linked by blood and marriage) で結ばれ

linked together by blood and marriage. People in the process of climbing into the higher rungs of society through business success, political power or other means make every effort to get their sons and daughters married into high society, an arrangement which will be advantageous to them.

The **gaku-batsu** is the alma mater clique. If a young man joins a company where men from his university are dominant, **gaku-batsu** sectarianism will favor him in promotions. On the other hand, if a person belongs to a minor **gaku-batsu** in the company, he has no chance of rising to a high executive position no matter how able he may be. In recent years, the **gaku-batsu** element has become less important in the business world, although it is still strongly entrenched in the bureaucracy and in academic circles.

Another one is **chihō-batsu**. This can be regarded as a form of sectionalism because **chihō** is a word which means district or region. Persons who come from the same region of the country are regarded as belonging to that area's **batsu**, and they tend to help and favor each other. However, thanks to the high demographic mobility of recent years, people are beginning to place less emphasis on this **batsu**.

Bōnasu

Japanese salaried workers receive extra wages

ている人びとである。事業で成功したり，政治権力その他の手段で社会の階層を昇りつめていく過程にある人びとは，自分の子女を良い家系に縁付かせようと必死になる。そうなってくれれば，万事好都合だからだ。

「学閥」は，同窓生仲間で作られる。新人の入った会社で，その出身大学の先輩が "幅" を利かしていれば，その人の昇進に有利となる。一方，その人の学閥が社内で勢力が小さければ，どんなに有能でも，上級管理職に昇進する見込みはまずない。しかし近年は，学閥もビジネスの世界ではそれほど決定的な要素ではなくなってきている。しかし，官界や学界では，まだ根強いようだ。

「地方閥」というものもある。この閥は一種の sectionalism と思われる。同じ地方出身者は，地方閥に属しているとみなされ，これらの人達は，たがいに助けあい，便宜をはかる。だが，近年は人口流動が激しいので，この閥もだんだん重視されなくなってきた。

ボーナス

日本のサラリーマンは，年に2回，ふつうは6/7月と12

in the form of a bonus, pronounced **bõnasu** by Japanese, twice a year, normally in June-July and December. The amount averages between one to three months' equivalent of the employee's monthly salary.

The bonus was originally a profit-sharing system. Before World War II, the management of a company which enjoyed good business during the preceding half-year period paid a large bonus (sometimes the equivalent of six months' salary or more). In bad times there was little or no bonus.

Today, workers regard the bonus as an integral part of their annual salary. They cover their day-to-day expenses with their monthly pay and use the bonus for buying expensive clothes and durable goods. A good part of the bonus is salted away for future expenses such as the children's education. This is one of the reasons why the Japanese savings rate is so high. Labor unions claim the bonus is a form of deferred payment of compensation to which the employee is entitled. Strikes over the amount of the bonus are not unusual.

Bõnen-kai and Shin·nen-kai

For Japanese businessmen, December is the

月に「ボーナス」の形で一時金をもらう。その額は，平均して月給の1カ月分から3カ月分である。

「ボーナス」は，そもそもは利益金分配制度であった。第2次大戦前は，会社の過去6カ月の業績が良いと，経営側は多額のボーナスを支給した（ときにはサラリーの6カ月以上ということさえあった）。業績不振だと，ボーナスはすずめの涙ほどかゼロであった。

ところが今日では「ボーナス」は給与の不可分の一部だ，と労働者はみなしている。日常の支払いは月給ですませ，高価な衣服とか耐久財をボーナスで買うのである。ボーナスのかなりの部分は，子供の教育費といった将来の出費に備えて貯金する。これが，日本人の貯蓄率の高い理由のひとつとなっている。労組は，ボーナスを一種の後払い賃金とみなしており，労働者の当然の権利だとする。ボーナス支給額をめぐってストライキをすることも珍しくない。

忘年会 と 新年会

日本のサラリーマンにとって12月は，「忘年会」という

month of the **bõnen-kai** office party. As the characters in the ideogram (forget-year-party) show, it is a function to wind up the year. Each section of a large company holds its own **bõnen-kai**, with every member chipping in to cover the cost. Because the year-end party is universal, tables in restaurants have to be reserved well in advance.

Alcohol flows freely because how else can the memories of the year's failures, frustrations, disappointments and irritations be washed down the river of time. Of course, the better, happier occasions are remembered with appropriate toasts.

With the past thus buried, or pickled in alcohol, everyone is ready to make a fresh start with the coming of the New Year. Some groups also hold a New Year party (**shin·nen-kai**), but usually they only have one or the other.

→ **Bureikõ**

Buchõ

The **buchõ** is the chief of a division, reporting to the managing director or the president of a company. Some **buchõ** are members of the board of directors.

The traditional Japanese job description of the **buchõ** is that he participates in intra-division meetings and chairs the intra-division meetings.

宴会の月である。Forget-year-party，読んで字のごとく，1年の締めくくりになる。大会社では，部課ごとに忘年会をやる。部課員はそれぞれに会費を出しあう。どこもかしこも年末パーティをやるので，かなり以前からレストランの席は予約しておかなければならない。

酒がたくさんでる。この1年間の失敗やら不満，落胆，苛立ちを，去りゆく時とともに洗い流してしまうには，酒しかあるまい。もちろん，良かったこと楽しかったことは，思い出しては乾杯する。過去を水に流したり，アルコール漬けにして，さて気分一新，新しい年の出発を迎えるのである。New-Year-party（新年会）をやるところもあるが，大体忘年会をやったら新年会をやらないというように，どちらか一方をやるのがふつうである。

→ 無礼講

部長

「部長」は chief of a division。会社の専務または社長に直属する。部長の一部は取締役である。日本では，部長職は，各部間の会議に出席したり，部内会議を主宰する。

The role of the **buchō** in the big companies is similar to that of the president of a member enterprise of a large American conglomerate, but the modus operandi is somewhat different.

For example, the **buchō** seldom dictates letters to his secretary. In fact, not many **buchō** have one. Instead, he tells one of his subordinates what kind of a letter needs to be sent out. The draft is written at a lower level and comes up for the **buchō**'s signature by way of the **kakarichō** (sub-section chief) and the **kachō** (section chief).

→ **Kachō**

Bureikō

Bureikō originally meant a meeting of people who were on intimate terms, regardless of rank. Nowadays, we hear this word at a New Year's party (**shin·nen-kai**), year-end party (**bōnen-kai**) and company excursion (**shain-ryokō**) in the form "Let's go **bureikō** today". This means "Let's leave aside rank and seniority today and have a good time drinking". In other words, it indicates that a lack of formality will be tolerated.

But even though there will be no standing on ceremony, people with organizational titles will still be addressed as "**Buchō**" or "**Jōmu**" instead of "— **san**".

→ **Bōnen-kai, Shain-ryokō, — San**

大会社の部長となると，その役割はアメリカの大コングロマリットの構成企業体の社長に匹敵するが，仕事のやり方はかなり異なる。部長が秘書に手紙を口述することはめったにない。事実，自分専属の秘書をもっている部長は，そうざらにはいない。そのかわり部長は部下に，こんな趣旨の手紙を出せ，と命ずる。手紙は下のレベルで起案され，係長（sub-section chief），課長（section chief）を経て，部長のところにあがってきて，部長の署名をもらってから出すという段取りである。

→ 課長

無礼講

上下の別なく親しみあう仲間の集まりが元の意味だが，新年会，忘年会，あるいは社内旅行の宴会などで，席上「今日は無礼講でいこう」などという。社内の序列・役職の上下の別なく飲もう，楽しもう，との意味につかわれる。席上で多少失礼なことがあっても，大目に見ようということである。しかし，無礼講ではあっても，役職者には「部長」とか「常務」と職名で呼びかけ，単に「—— さん」と呼びかけることはあまりない。

→ 忘年会と新年会，社員旅行，—— さん

— Chon (Saka-chon, etc.)

—Chon is used to describe a **tanshin-funin** person who goes to take up a regional post to which he has been assigned but leaves his family behind for reasons such as the schooling of his children. (The number of people who choose **tanshin-funin** because their wives are working still seems to be few.)

The first part of the Korean word "chongak", which means "bachelor", is adopted and prefixed with the corrupted name of the place to which the person is assigned. For example, **Saka-chon** refers to a person who is assigned to Osaka but left his family behind in Tokyo, etc. **Nago-chon** is "a bachelor in Nagoya" and **Satchon** "a bachelor in Sapporo". It is a word which is redolent with the loneliness of the **tanshin-funin.**

→ **Shain-ryõ, Tanshin-funin**

Chõrei

At many Japanese factories and offices, the working day begins with **chõrei.** This traditional institution, a source of amazement for westerners, is something like a morning pep talk.

In some companies, the president gives a brief talk. In large companies, each section holds its own **chõrei**, with the section manager giving the pep talk. At some offices, the workers go

—— チョン

　地方転勤を命ぜられた家族もちのサラリーマンが，子供の進学などの都合で（まだ共働き主婦の勤務の都合は少ないようだが）家族を残して「単身赴任」（同項参照）する場合などにつかわれる。韓国語で独身男性を意味するチョンガーのチョンに地方名の一部をかぶせて呼ばれる。たとえば東京に家族を残し大阪に単身赴任する人を「阪チョン」，以下同様に名古屋「名古チョン」，札幌「札チョン」のごとくである。単身赴任のわびしさをしのばせることばでもある。

　→ 社員寮，単身赴任

朝礼

　日本の工場や職場では，朝礼とともに1日の仕事を始めるところが多い。この昔からの制度（欧米の人にはなんとも奇妙に映る）は一種の morning pep talk である。会社によっては，社長みずから短い訓話をする。大会社では，部課ごとに朝礼をやり，部課長が激励の訓辞をする。職場

through a set of limbering-up exercises and finish off by singing the company song or shouting the company slogan in unison.

The meeting lasts only a few minutes, but it helps create a "let's go" mood and a feeling of identity with the group. **Chõrei** is usually held every morning, but some companies schedule it only for the first day of the week. It's effective in shaking off those Monday morning blues.

→ **Shaka, Shaze**

Chotto

In a shop, you want to get the assistant to serve you. In a restaurant, you want to call the waiter's attention. You don't need to feel lost for words. All you have to say is **chotto**. In the street, you want to ask a stranger the way. Your opening gambit can be **chotto**.

For a Japanese, it would be impolite to accost a stranger in the street with **chotto**. But for the visitor from abroad, it is not only acceptable but also somewhat charming if it is said with a sweet, genial or forlorn expression.

For another reason, also, **chotto** is one of the first words that anyone coming to Japan from overseas learns. **Chotto matte** is "one moment please" or "wait! " whether on the phone or anywhere else.

→ **Sumimasen**

によっては，軽い体操などもやり，締めくくりに社歌の合唱や会社の信条を唱和する。朝礼は2，3分程度で終わるが，"やる気"を起こさせ，一体感を生み出す。朝礼は毎朝行なうのがふつうだが，週の初日だけやるところもある。これは"月曜の朝の憂鬱病"（Monday morning blues）を吹き飛ばす効果がある。

→ 社歌，社是，社訓

ちょっと

お店で店員を呼びたいとき，レストランで給仕にきてもらいたいとき，「さて，なんといったらよいのか？」などとあれこれ思い悩むことはない。「ちょっと」といえば，万事こと足りる。見知らぬ人に道を尋ねるときまず最初に「ちょっと」である。

日本人が表で見も知らぬ人に「ちょっと」と呼びかけるのは失礼になることもある。しかし外国から来た人ならかまわない。それどころか，やんわりと，明るく，あるいは困った表情でいえば，チャーミングでさえある。また，別の理由から，海外から日本に来た人が最初に覚えることばのひとつも「ちょっと」である。「ちょっと待て」は"one moment please"ないし"wait"で，電話でもほかでもつかえる重宝なことばである。

→ すみません

Chotto ippai

On the surface of it, **chotto ippai** means "let's have a quick drink". It is one of the most frequently heard expressions among company staff members at the end of the day's work, but it does not mean they are alcohol lovers. It's because sitting down together for a drink after work and before going home for dinner gives salaried workers a chance to exchange information and opinions.

The boss suggests **chotto ippai** to a subordinate when he wants to admonish him privately or to hear his suggestions and complaints. In a way, it's an informal extension of work.

The place chosen for **chotto ippai** is usually an inexpensive drinking establishment. **Chotto ippai**, therefore, is an institution which lubricates human relations among businessmen.

→ **Aka-chōchin**

Dame-oshi

Dame-oshi is the name given to the process of making something doubly sure.

ちょっと一杯

　直訳すると，「ちょっと一杯」は，"Let's have a quick drink." の意味であるが，1日の仕事がひけたとき，職場仲間で一番よく耳にすることばでもある。"のんべえ" だからではない。仕事が終わり，家に帰って夕食をとるまえに，仲間と一緒に飲めば，情報の交換やら，不平不満をぶつけることができる。ボスが部下に内々で注意したいときとか，部下の意見や苦情を聞いてみようと思うとき，「ちょっと一杯」と誘う。いいかえれば，非公式な仕事の延長でもある。

　ちょっと一杯をやるところは，たいていは安上がりの飲み屋である。こんなわけで，「ちょっと一杯」は，サラリーマンの人間関係に潤滑油の役を果たすものとでもいえようか。

　→ 赤ちょうちん

だめ押し

　「だめ押し」は英語で "making something doubly sure" である。仕事の話で夕食会の招待を受けたとする。その当

You accept an invitation to a business dinner. On the day of the dinner, you get a call from your host's secretary to confirm your attendance. You promise to deliver goods on a certain date. A few days before the scheduled time, the customer inquires if he can still expect delivery on that date. A decision has been reached at a meeting. Some time later, those who attended the meeting are asked to reconfirm the decision.

All these are instances of **dame-oshi**. This kind of reminding and reconfirming sometimes irritates the Westerner, but in Japanese society **dame-oshi** is an accepted practice which ensures that things will go smoothly as previously arranged, decided, or promised. **Dame-oshi** reduces the possibility of last-minute hitches.

Dochira-e?

Very often you will hear Japanese greeting each other on the street with "**Dochira-e?** ", which literally means "Where are you going? "

It is not a sign that the Japanese are inquisitive about the destination of someone they happen to meet on the street. It should not be taken as prying into one's private affairs, because it is only a way of greeting, and means no more than a cheery "hello".

If a Japanese is asked "**Dochira-e?** " by an acquaintance, he will not take it for a definite

日，招待側の秘書から電話がかかってきて，出席をあらた
めて確認する。これこれの日に品物を届ける約束をする。
配達予定日の2，3日前に，お客から約束の配達日に変更
はないかどうか問いあわせてくる。会議である事項が決ま
った。しばらくして，この会議に出席した人達は，決定事
項の再確認を求められる。

　これらはすべて，だめ押しの例である。この種の注意喚
起なり再確認は，欧米の人には煩雑に思えるかもしれない
が，日本ではだめ押しはあたり前のこととされている。事
前の取決め，決定ないし約束どおりに物事を円滑に運ぶた
めである。だめ押ししておけば，間際になって手違いの起
こるおそれは少なくなる。

どちらへ？

　道で出会った人がおたがいに「どちらへ」と挨拶するの
をよく耳にする。直訳すると "Where are you going ?"
である。道でひょっこり出会った人に行き先を聞きたがる
ほど好奇心がつよいわけではない。他人のプライバシーに
立ち入ったことだ，などと解釈してはいけない。なぜなら
ほんの挨拶なのであって "Hello" ぐらいの意味しかない
のだから。

　日本人は，知りあいの人から「どちらへ」と聞かれたか
らといって，行き先を聞かれているとはとらない。とくに

question and will probably just give a vague reply, unless he particularly wants to specify where he is going. When a foreigner is addressed by a Japanese friend on the street **"Dochira-e?"**, he should not feel offended but simply reply with the stock greeting **"chotto soko made"** (just over there), with an ambiguous smile.

Dōki

"How's your business compared with last year?" "Well, in the first half of this year we managed to increase our sales by five percent over **dōki** last year." Here the word means "same period" or "corresponding period" a functional expression which is indispensable in talking about business performance.

"Mr. Yamada is the first among his **dōki** to become a director of the company." Although the word is written with the same Chinese characters as in the first example, it wouldn't make sense if rendered into English as "same period". Used in this sense **dōki** is redolent with meaning. It refers to persons who entered the company in the same year as Mr. Yamada.

This **dōki** relationship is very much emphasized in Japanese organizations where promotion is by seniority and personnel officers make an effort to treat all **dōki** equally in giving promotions or assignments. **Dōki** persons in a company often

行き先をいいたいときは別だが，たいていは「ちょっとそこまで」といってあいまいな答えをする。外国人が往来で日本人の友人から「どちらへ」と聞かれても，失礼と思わずに，あいまいな笑みを浮かべて「ちょっとそこまで」（just over there）と答えればよろしい。

同期

「去年とくらべて業績はどう？」「まあ，上半期はどうやら，昨年同期比5パーセント増にはこぎつけたけどね。」ここにいう「同期」とは same period とか corresponding period など，おたがいを比較するのにつかわれる用語で，業績の話をするときかならずつかわれる。

「山田さんは，同期のトップを切って重役になった。」この場合の「同期」は，漢字では上記の例と同じだが，だからといって英語でも同じに same period と訳したのでは，なんのことかさっぱり分からない。ここにいう「同期」とは意味がいささか違い，山田さんと同じ年に入社した人達を指す。この「同期」の関係は，日本の組織体ではきわめて重視される。昇進は年功序列制がふつうなので，昇進または配置転換のばあい，人事担当は，同期の人みんなを同等に扱うよう努力する。会社の同期生は，情報交換したり

39

hold informal meetings of their own to compare notes and maintain contact.

Dõmo

Dõmo, which means "very", "much" or "indeed", is a versatile colloquial word. In everyday conversation, it prefaces such words as **arigatõ** (thank you) and **sumimasen** (sorry).

When the situation makes it obvious whether you mean thank you or sorry or welcome, the operative word is often dropped and only **dõmo** is used. When repeated in succession "**dõmo-dõmo**", it has the effect of expressing greater feeling or enthusiasm.

A salesman may introduce himself to a customer with a **dõmo**, have his order book signed and say **dõmo** and leaves with another **dõmo**. The use of **dõmo** alone is not as polite as the full expression **dõmo arigatõ**.

Dõsõsei

Old school relationships play an important role in the Japanese business and social world. The simple fact that two businessmen have known each other since college days or even just went to the same school is often enough to open a new account between two firms, expedite contracts or arrange the informal exchange of business tips which are otherwise difficult to obtain.

接触を保つために，よく仲間うちだけで非公式な集まりを
持つ。

どうも

　「どうも」とは very, much とか indeed の意味で，なに
にでも使える日常語である。日常の会話で「どうもありが
とう」（Thank you），「どうもすみません」（Sorry）と
いったように，ありがとう，すみません，などの前につける。
前後の関係から，ありがとう，すみません，ようこそ，の
意味だと明らかに分かるときには，本体を省いて，ただ「ど
うも」とだけいうことがよくある。「どうもどうも」とつ
づけて繰り返すと，強く感じている気持ちないし熱意をあ
らわす効果をもつ。

　セールスマンが，まず「どうも」といってお客を訪問し，
注文書に署名をもらうと，「どうも」といい，帰るとき，ま
た「どうも」という。「どうも」だけですますのは，「どう
もありがとう」などと，ちゃんと最後までいうのにくらべ
ると，多少礼儀にかけていることになるが。

同窓生

　日本では，学生時代の関係が，仕事の面でもつきあいの
上でも，重要な役割を果たす。商談で2人が，たまたま大
学時代からずっと知っているとか，同じ学校の「同窓生」
だと分かると，それだけで会社同士の新しい取引に道が開
けたり，買付契約がすらすら運んだり，ふつうならなかな
か手に入らないビジネス上の情報も非公式に交換できる。

Japanese businessmen therefore go to great pains to maintain their **dōsōsei** (alumni) network. Class reunions are held frequently and alumni bulletins are circulated to keep the old school ties together. This is an example of a horizontal relationship in Japanese business society, which otherwise tends to be structured vertically.

→ **Dōki, Batsu**

Futokoro-gatana

In the English-speaking world, if you should liken a man to a dagger, it is not complimentary. Although the original meaning of **futokoro-gatana** is dagger or dirk, it is well regarded for a person to be described as such in Japan. This is because, in reference to a person, it is used to mean a confidant or right-hand man.

This meaning comes from the fact that in feudal Japan people carried the dagger in the **futokoro** = bosom. It was an instrument for committing **hara-kiri** in order to defend one's honor.

From this, the word took on today's meaning that it is a man who is privy to the secret plans of a person holding a responsible position or one who is most trusted by such a person. In other

だから日本のビジネスマンは，なんとかして「同窓生」（alumni）のつながりを保っておこうとする。昔の学校時代のきずなを断たないように，クラス会がひんぱんに開かれ，同窓会報も配布される。日本のビジネス社会は，本来タテ型の構造になりがちだが，これはヨコ型の関係の一例である。

　→ 同期，閥

懐刀（ふところがたな）

　英語圏で，人をあいくちなどにたとえても，あまり褒めたことにならないだろう。もともと「懐刀」とは，あいくちとか短刀のことだが，日本では，これになぞらえられると重要視されたことになる。人に対しては腹心の部下とか右腕の意味でつかわれるからである。これは，封建時代の日本で「懐」（bosom）に短刀を携えていたところからきたものである。この短刀は，名誉を護るために切腹するときの道具でもあった。

　ここから，「懐刀」ということばは今日一般につかわれて

words, the **futokoro-gatana** is a sort of chief of staff and the right hand of a person in high position.

Gakureki

One of the changes taking place in Japanese society today is the attitude towards the **gakureki** or school background. It used to be that a person's **gakureki** inevitably shaped his course in professional life.

It is only a slight exaggeration to say that, if a person had graduated from the "right" university, his career all the way to the top was just about automatically charted for him. Conversely, no matter how capable, the man who did not come from the "right" school had little chance to reach the top. This fact of life made young men seek university education in droves.

Today, with more and more people having the benefit of university education and business having become increasingly competitive, less importance is beginning to be placed on **gakureki.** If he does not have real business ability, a man who comes from a name university can be surpassed by one from a lesser known institution.

→ **Batsu, Dōsōsei**

Gashi-kōkan

For several days after business offices reopen

いる。責任ある地位の人の内密な計画を知っている人，または，このような責任ある人に信用されている腹心的存在の人を指す。いいかえれば，「懐刀」とは，偉い人の参謀またはブレインといった役どころの人である。

学歴

日本で近頃変わってきたことのひとつに「学歴」（school background）に対する考え方がある。かつては，その人の学歴で，社会に出てからのコースが決まってしまった。おおげさにいえば，"いい大学"を卒業していれば，トップに昇進する道がおのずから開けているようなものだった。逆に，どんなに能力があろうとも"いい学校"を出ていないと，トップにつくチャンスはまずなかった。このため若い人は，ねこもしゃくしも大学を目指した。

ところが今日では，大学卒の肩書をもっている人が増える一方だし，企業も次第に競争が激しくなってきたので，学歴は以前ほど重視されないようになり始めている。仕事ができなければ，一流大学出でも，さして有名でもない学校の出身者に追いこされてしまうのである。

→閥，同窓生

賀詞交換

三箇日がすぎ，仕事始めになると，数日間というもの，

after the New Year holidays, businessmen are busy attending **gashi-kōkan** parties. These are functions at which people gather to exchange New Year's greetings and to ask each other's favor during the coming year. Most of these functions are sponsored by industrial associations and are usually scheduled during the daytime.

Gashi-kōkan is a very convenient function because it eliminates the necessity for businessmen to make time-consuming individual rounds to wish each other a Happy New Year. It has a very special atmosphere because participants make determined attempts to meet as many people as possible to exchange greetings.

The function is also known as **meishi-kōkan** which means "exchanging visiting cards". During the period of **gashi-kōkan** parties, businessmen are excused for sitting at their desks flushed with alcohol.

→ **Aisatsu-mawari, Meishi**

Gebahyō

Although the standard Japanese-English dictionary gives "rumor" and "gossip" as the English equivalents of **gebahyō**, the Japanese word is usually used with a nuance not contained in the given English equivalents.

It is most frequently used to mean "speculation among outsiders concerning the possible outcome

「賀詞交換」で忙しい。ビジネスマンが一堂に会して，新年の挨拶を交わし，「本年もどうぞよろしく」と頭を下げる。賀詞交換のパーティは，業種団体主催のばあいが多く，たいていは日中に行なわれる。

賀詞交換会は，とても便利である。1人ずつ個別に回って，「新年おめでとう」と挨拶して歩く時間が省ける。参会者ができるだけ多くの人に挨拶しようと血眼になっているから，会場には一種独特の雰囲気がある。このパーティは「名刺交換会」ともいう。exchanging visiting card の意味である。賀詞交換会がつづいている期間は，オフィスでアルコールの匂いをプンプンさせても大目にみてもらえる。

→ 挨拶まわり，名刺

下馬評

ふつうの和英辞典で下馬評をひくと rumor とか gossip とある。しかし，このことばは，英語にないニュアンスでつかわれるのがふつうである。すなわち「これから起ることや行事ないし過程についてのうわさ話。ほとんどが人

of an event or proceedings, relating mostly to personnel matters". Thus, "the **gebahyō** at Kabuto-cho (Japan's Wall Street) is that Mr. A will be selected over Mr. B as the next president of Company X".

The origin of the word goes back to the days when retainers waiting for their lords at the horse-dismounting (**geba**) place outside a castle or a shrine or temple, engaged in idle speculation about personnel changes in the Shogunate government.

Gokurō-sama, Otsukare-sama

The word **gokurō-sama** means "I appreciate your labor" or "Thank you for your trouble" or sometimes "I sympathize with you for your tough assignment". When the word is said to someone going off to attend to a task, it can carry the meaning of "Good luck!" Thus it is an expression which can be said to a person who is setting off for work, who is in the process of performing a task, or who has finished a job or returned from work.

Otsukare-sama is said to a person who has completed a job. It means "It must have been tiring" and expresses gratitude. The businessman returning home from work is greeted by his wife with **otsukare-sama** or **gokurō-sama**.

→ **Shitsurei shimasu**

事関係のうわさ話」の意味につかう。だから「兜町（日本版ウォール街）の下馬評だと，Ｘ社の次期社長にはＢ氏を抜いてＡ氏が選任されるだろう」といったつかい方をする。語源は，江戸時代，城，神社，寺院の外の下馬地域で，供待ちが幕府高官の人事異動について，たわいもない臆測をしたことに溯る。

ご苦労さま，お疲れさま

「ご苦労さま」とは，"I appreciate your labor" とか "Thank you for your trouble" ときには "sympathize with you for your tough assignment" の意味である。これから仕事にとりかかろうという人にいうときには，"Good luck" の意味ともなる。つまり，これから仕事を始める人，仕事をしている最中の人，仕事を終えた人，あるいは勤めから帰宅した人など，いろいろにつかわれる。

「お疲れさま」は仕事を終えた人にいう。"It must have been tiring" の意味で，感謝をあらわす。勤めを終えて帰宅した夫に，妻は「お疲れさま」あるいは「ご苦労さま」とことばをかける。

→ 失礼します

Gomasuri

You find him in every organization and every society. He may not be a bad fellow but his colleagues do not speak well of him. More often than not, he is looked upon with contempt except usually by the person on whom he practices his technique.

In the English-speaking world, the **gomasuri** is known as the "apple polisher". A high-sounding name for him is "sycophant", a self-seeking person who courts favor in a servile manner by flattering others. The literal translation of the Japanese word is "a person who grinds sesame seeds".

Roasted sesame seeds are ground in an earthenware mortar to make flavoring for Japanese-style dishes. In the grinding process, the seeds fly in all directions and stick to the wall of the mortar almost in a cringing way.

Thus, the noun **gomasuri** — apple polisher or apple polishing — and the verb **goma wo suru** — to flatter or toady, figuratively, of course.

ごますり

　この種の人間は，どの組織，どの社会にもいる。悪い奴
ではないのだろうが，彼のことを同僚はよくいわない。た
いていは軽蔑の眼でみられる。ごまをすられている人は別
だ。英語圏では，「ごますり」は apple polisher である。
おおげさにいえば sycophant のこと。つまり相手におべ
っかをつかって，卑屈な態度で気に入られようとする利己
主義者のこと。「ごますり」を直訳すると a person who
grinds sesame seeds ということになる。

　日本料理に風味をつけるため，煎った「ごま」をすりば
ちですって利用する。この「ごま」は，すられているうち
に，種子が四方に散って，すり鉢の内壁にべったりと付着
する。

　このように，名詞は「ごますり」——apple polisher と
か apple polishing。動詞の「ごまをする」は，to flatter
or toady となる。

Goshūgi

One of the characteristics of Japanese society is the way people observe formalities and conventions, some of which might appear irrational to the Western mind. One of these is **goshūgi**. **Go** is an honorific prefix and **shūgi** means "celebration or congratulation"

This is carried over into the business world when one gives a **goshūgi torihiki** or when we have a **goshūgi sõba**. The former is a transaction made not because of its business merits but in order to express congratulations to a person or company just starting a business.

The latter is generally used to describe the buoyant prices on the stock exchange on the first business day of the New Year. New Year's is a felicitous time, and it just won't do to have a slumping market, no matter what the realities. Thus, buyers and sellers usually cooperate to give the market a boost when it reopens for business after the New Year holidays.

Hada

Hada is skin, but in Japanese expressions it is not only used in its base meaning, but also to mean temperament, character, disposition, bent, type, mold, etc.

ご祝儀

　形式やしきたりを守ることが日本社会の特徴である。欧米の人からみると、これら形式やしきたりのなかには、不合理に思えるものもあるかもしれない。そのひとつが「ご祝儀」である。「ご」は敬語をあらわす接頭語、「祝儀」は、celebration とか congratulation の意。

　ビジネスの世界では、「ご祝儀取引」とか「ご祝儀相場」などとつかわれる。前者は商売上のうまみがあるからではなく、開業したばかりの人や企業に対するお祝いを表わすために取引することである。後者は、年明けの株式市場の大発会で、市場がにぎわうことをいう。年の始めはおめでたい時なので、現実はどうであれ、不景気なスタートを切りたくないからである。そこで買手も売手も協力して、年明けの仕事始めには、株価にはずみをつけるのである。

肌

　「肌」は skin。比喩に使うと、temperament（気質）、character（性格）、disposition（性癖）、bent（好み）, type（型）、mold（たち）といった意味である。かならずしも、品の悪い意味ではない。

Hada-zawari means feel or touch, as in soft or rough touch. In reference to a person, we say **hada-zawari ga yawarakai** (soft). This means that the person is gentle-mannered, affable, courteous.

Hada ni awanai is "not suitable or agreeable to the skin". From this, it is a polite way of saying that one doesn't like a certain person. It also means that two persons are not compatible with each other or cannot get along with each other because of personality, ideology, taste or interests. If someone feels uncomfortable in a certain post because it doesn't suit his temperament, he can say that it's a **hada ni awanai** position for him. This would mean that he feels like a fish out of water. The opposite is **hada ni au**. (→ **Ki ni iru**)

When one wants to say a certain person is a scholarly type or has an academic bent, the expression **hada** is used. The statement would be "he is **gakusha-hada**". **Gakusha** (scholar) can be replaced with politician (**seiji-ka**), merchant (**shōnin**), scientist (**kagaku-sha**), diplomat (**gaikōkan**), artist (**geijutsu-ka**), etc.

Hai and Ĩe

Hai is yes and **ĩe** is no. That sounds simple. However, unfortunately for international communications, the Japanese **hai** does not always have the same meaning as the English "yes". To

「肌ざわり」といえば，feel（感触）とか touch（触覚）。肌にふれた感じが硬いとかやわらかいこと。人にいうときには，「肌ざわりがやわらかい」（soft）という。gentle-mannered（物腰のおだやかな），affable（丁寧な），courteous（丁重な）人をいう。

「肌に合わない」とは，not suitable or agreeable to the skin（なんとなく，気持ちが合わない）こと。あの人は好きじゃない，ということの遠回しないい方。また，二人が互いにぴったりしないこと，性格や物の考え方，好み，興味などの違いから，一緒にやってゆけないことも「肌に合わない」である。あるポストが自分の性分に合わなくて，いやだいやだと思っているばあい，そのポストは，「肌に合わない」のである。勝手が違って本領が発揮できない（a fish out of water）と思っている意味。その反対は「肌に合う」である。（→気に入る）

あの人は学者タイプ（scholarly type）だとか，学問に向いている（academic bent）といいたければ，肌がつかわれる。たとえば，「学者肌」だというように。学者を別の言葉におきかえてもよい。「政治家肌」「商人肌」「科学者肌」「外交官肌」「芸術家肌」など。

はいといいえ

「はい」は yes，「いいえ」は no である。実に簡単明瞭なことなのだが，国際間のコミュニケーションにおいて，残念ながら日本語の「はい」は，かならずしも英語の yes

55

the question "He does not speak Japanese, does he?" the Japanese answer "**hai**" would mean the same as the English answer "no" and vice versa.

The Japanese often carry over into English their peculiar usage of **hai** and **ĩe**, causing misunderstanding and confusion. Another problem that arises in connection with **ĩe** is that the Japanese tend to avoid using it. They don't want to embarrass or hurt the other party by refuting, denying or rejecting.

The safest way for the foreign businessman dealing with Japanese is not to accept a "yes" or a "no" as an answer but to persuade them to phrase the answer in a sentence.

Hanko

Without this instrument, which is slightly thicker than a pencil and about five centimeters long, business in Japan would quickly come to a standstill. The **hanko**, or seal, is used in place of one's personal signature.

Most corporate decisions must await the completion of the process whereby documents have been read and approved, then stamped with the **hanko** of all those concerned. This process rarely results in hasty decisions. The seal businessmen use in signing routine papers is usually a

の意味とはかぎらない。"He does not speak Japanese, does he ?" という質問に、日本人が「はい」と答えたら、英語の no と同じ意味である。その逆もまたいえる。

　日本人は、その独特の「はい」と「いいえ」のつかい方を英語にもちこむので、誤解や混乱が起きる。もうひとつの問題は、日本人は no をつかうことをさけたがることである。断ったり、否定したり、拒否したりして、相手を困らせたり、傷つけたくない、という思いやりがあるからだ。

　外国のビジネスマンが、日本人と相対するときは、ただ yes とか no だけの答えでわかったと思わず、yes または no のあとに続く文章も完全にいってもらうことである。これが誤解を防ぐもっとも安全な方法である。

はんこ

　鉛筆よりやや太目、長さ5センチほどのこの道具がないことには、日本で商売はたちどころに行き詰まってしまう。「はんこ」つまり seal が署名代わりにつかわれる。

　たいていの企業の決定は、文書を読み、承認し、それから関係者全員がはんこをつくまでは、完了しない。この手続きのために、早急な決定はしにくい。ビジネスマンがきまりきった書類に押すときに使う印鑑は、たいていは三文

san·mon-ban which is ready-made and available at stationery stores.

Hanko is shortened to **han** and is sometimes pronounced **ban** when used in combination with another word, such as **san·mon-ban**.

→ **Ringi**

Hara

Anatomically, **hara** is the abdomen or stomach. Used in figures of speech, the word can mean the heart or the mind of a man but not of a woman. **Hara** appears in a large number of expressions.

The author who devoted a whole book to **hara-gei** (stomach art) would probably say that it is presumptions to try to explain in just a few lines this Japanese problem - solving technique. **Hara-gei** may be explained as a technique for solving a problem through negotiation between two individuals without the use of direct words. You don't reveal to the other party what is in your

判。出来あいで，文具店で買える代物である。

「はんこ」は短くして「はん」（判）という。「三文判」の
ように，他の言葉と組み合わせたとき，「ばん」と発音す
ることがある。

→稟議

腹

　解剖学上からいうと「腹」はabdomen または stomach。
これを比喩的につかうと，男性の心とか考えの意味になる。
女性にはつかわない。腹に関しいろいろな言いまわしがあ
る。

　「腹芸」（stomach art）を主題に1冊の本を著した人
にいわせれば，この日本式問題解決法をわずか数行で説明
するなどは，おこがましいことであろう。「腹芸」とは，2
人の間の交渉で，直接，ことばに出さずに問題を解決して
しまう技術とでもいったらよい。腹の内にあるものを相手
に明かさなくとも，目的なり，願望，要求，意図，忠告な

hara but you unmistakably and effectively communicate your purpose, desire, demand, intention, advice or whatever through **hara-gei**.

To do this, you bring into play psychology, intuition and your knowledge of the other party's personality, background, ambitions, personal connections, etc. and also what the other party knows about you. Only people with plenty of experience and cool nerves can make it succeed, but a lot of communication between Japanese in high positions is through **hara-gei**. (→ **Ishin-den-shin**)

Hara wo watte hanasu (to cut open the stomach and talk) = to have a heart-to-heart talk

Hara wo miseru (to show the stomach) = to reveal what is in one's mind

Hara wo kukuru (to bundle up the stomach) = to become resigned to something or resolve to do something whatever the outcome

Hara-guroi (the stomach is black) = a treacherous person, a schemer

Seppuku = to cut open the stomach. **Puku** is another way of reading the character for **hara**. This is the proper word for the act which has become known in the outside world as **hara-kiri**. **Seppuku** was the honorable course given to the feudal warrior in place of execution. It is an act whose purpose is to show that one's **hara** is clean. (→ **Futokoro gatana**)

ど，間違いなく，効果的にコミュニケートするのが腹芸である。そのためには，心理，直観，相手の個性，背景，狙い，個人的なつながり，それに相手がこちらをどの程度知っているか，といったいろいろの要素が必要だ。経験豊かで，冷静な神経の持ち主にして初めてうまくできることである。高い地位にある日本人同士のコミュニケーションは腹芸によることが多い。(→以心伝心)

「腹を割って話す」(to cut open the stomach and talk) = to have a heart-to-heart talk

「腹をみせる」(to show the stomach) = to reveal what is in one's mind

「腹をくくる」(to bundle up the stomach)= become resigned to or to resolve to (あきらめる，決心する)

「腹黒い」(stomach is black)= a treacherous person, a schemer (策士)

「切腹」(腹を切る)は，外国で"はらきり"といわれている行為の正式名称である。切腹とは，封建時代に，処刑に代わり武士に与えられた名誉ある刑であった。これは，切腹するものが，自分の腹はきれいなんだということを証明するための行為であった。(→懐刀)

Tsume-bara wo kiru. This means **seppuku** which one does not want to do but which one cannot avoid. When the people around a person conspire to place that person in a situation where he just has to **seppuku**, it is called **tsume-bara wo kiraseru**. This expression is used in contemporary society when the people around force a person into a position where he has no recourse but to resign from his post or organization.

Jibara wo kiru (to cut one's own stomach) = to pay for something out of one's own pocket.

Hijikake-isu

When you walk into a Japanese office, you can tell who outranks whom by noticing the type of chair they are sitting in. The chair most coveted by company employees is the **hijikake-isu**, a large one with arm rests. The rank-and-file sit in the simplest of functional office chairs. They are not chairs for resting but for working.

When a person is promoted to the first rung of the managerial ladder, he gets a chair with an arm rest and quite often a bigger desk. As he goes up the ladder, he is given an increasingly larger and more comfortable **hijikake-isu**. When he gets to a leather-upholstered chair with high back rest, he is a director or perhaps the president. It's a chair for sitting back and thinking.

「詰め腹を切る」は，意志に反して，無理に腹を切らされることをいう。廻りの者たちが，ある人物を切腹せざるをえないような状況に追いこんだとき，その人物に「詰め腹を切らせる」という。今日では，周囲の人達がよってたかって，無理に辞任を強いるときに，この言葉がつかわれる。

　「自腹を切る」（ to cut one's own stomach ）とは，自分の小遣いから支払うことをいう。

肱かけ椅子

　日本のオフィスに入ると，座っている人の椅子をみれば，どの人がどの人より偉いか，すぐ分かる。サラリーマンが一度は座りたいと思っているのが，肱かけ椅子である。平社員はもっとも機能的な事務椅子に座る。休憩する椅子ではなく，働く椅子である。

　管理職への階段の第1段を昇ると，肱かけがついた椅子と，しばしば今迄より一回り大きい机が与えられる。昇進してゆくにつれて，肱かけ椅子はだんだんと大きく，座り心地のいいものになってゆく。皮張りで，うしろに寄りかかれる椅子に手が届いたときには，重役か社長である。どっかりとよりかかり，物を考える椅子である。

Hikinuki

In the Japanese corporation, the recruiting of personnel is, as a rule, conducted only once a year when young men graduate from the universities or high schools in spring. Persons who have worked in other companies are not usually hired. The exception is **ama-kudari**, a system under which companies take in retiring government officials to fill executive posts.

However, on the rare occasion, when a company urgently needs a person with a highly specialized talent or experience, it scouts other organizations to find a suitable man to persuade him to change jobs. This is called **hikinuki**, literally "to extract" or "to pluck out".

→ **Ama-kudari, Chūto-saiyō**

Hiru-andon

Hiru-andon translates as "a lamp in broad daylight". In broad daylight one cannot tell whether a lamp has been lit or not. From this fact, the word is used to refer to a person whose presence or existence is not regarded as important or to describe a person when it is difficult to determine whether he has value or not. However, it does not mean a person who is slow to react (such a person is called **keikōtō** = fluorescent lamp, which takes time to light up) or is mediocre.

引き抜き

日本の会社では，社員採用は原則として年に一度，大学や高校の卒業期に合わせて行なわれる。ほかの会社に勤めたことのある人は採用しないのがふつうである。例外は天下りである。これは退官した役人を重役などに迎える仕組みである。

しかし，まれに，高度の特殊技能なり，経験のある人を至急に必要とするとき，会社は，他の会社にあたって，然るべき人物を見つけ，転社を勧誘することがある。これを「引き抜き」という。読んで字のごとく extract とか pluck out の意味である。

→ 天下り，中途採用

昼あんどん

日中の「あんどん」の意味である。陽光下での「あんどん」は灯いているかいないかわからないところから，その人の存在価値が重視されないような人，またはその人の真価があるのかないのか解らない人のことをいう。ただし反応の遅い人（点灯の遅いところから「蛍光灯」という）とか，凡愚の人の意味ではない。

In many cases a Japanese organization operates better when its head is a person who does not stand out but who has a **kiremono** (sharp and able man) as his **futokoro-gatana** or chief of staff. In such a case, the top man is a symbol and the deputy or chief of staff holds the responsibility. Often, there are a plural number of deputies and/ or staff officers, so it does not happen that power becomes concentrated in one person. Perhaps this perception of the organization which has existed in Japan since the old days has prevented the emergence of a dictator.

Consequently, **hiru-andon** is not necessarily a deprecating reference and **kiremono** is not necessarily a word of praise.

→ **Futokoro-gatana**

Hon·ne and Tatemae

"That man doesn't disclose his **hon·ne** (real intentions) easily" is an expression Japanese businessmen use when talking about a tough negotiator on the other side. Your counterpart in a business negotiation may not be obstinate because he wants to be, but because, under certain circumstances, he has to emphasize his company's **tatemae** (principles or official stance).

When the **tatemae** and the **hon·ne** are the same, there is no problem. But sometimes it

日本の組織では，このように一見ぼんやりとした様子の人を長とし，有能な「切れ者」を懐刀ないし参謀として運営すると，ことがうまく運ぶことが多い。このばあいトップは象徴であり，副ないし参謀が結果についての責任を負うことになるし，副ないし参謀も複数であることが多いから，特定個人に権力が集中することは少ない。すなわち独裁者が生まれないのは，こうした組織感覚が日本には昔からあったからであろう。

　したがって「昼あんどん」とは，かならずしも人をおとしめたことにもならないし，「切れ者」は，かならずしも褒めたことばとはならないのである。

　→ 懐刀

本音 と 建前

　"あの人はなかなか「本音」(real intentions) をいわない" とは，商談で手ごわい相手について日本のビジネスマンがつかう表現である。交渉相手は，なにもそうしたいから頑張っているのではなく，会社の「建前」(principles または official stance) を力説せねばならないために譲ろうとしないのである。

　「建前」と「本音」が同じであれば，なにも問題はない。

happens that they are at variance with each other. The negotiation then becomes an exercise in trying to find a way to satisfy the **hon·ne** without compromising the **tatemae**, at least on the surface.

Excessive adherence to **tatemae**, of course, is often used as a ploy to gain a better bargaining position. The reluctance to reveal the **hon·ne** and to stick ostensibly to **tatemae** also occurs in private social relations, especially when the **hon·ne** is not a very laudable one.

Ishin-denshin

Ishin-denshin is communication of thought without the medium of words. The expression means "what the mind thinks, the heart transmits". In other societies, particularly Western, communication generally has to be expressed in specific words to be thoroughly understood. To the Westerner, therefore, the Japanese sometimes seem to have telepathic powers because so often communication among Japanese is achieved without the use of words.

ところが往々にして，この2つが食い違っていることがある。そのばあい，少なくとも表面上は「建前」を崩さずに「本音」を満たす方策を見つけることが交渉術になる。もちろん，かけ引きの立場を有利にする手として，建前に過度にこだわることもある。本音を明かさずに，表面上，建前に固執するというのは，個人のつきあいでもよくあることだ。本音があまり見上げたものでないときは，よけいにその傾向がつよい。

以心伝心

「以心伝心」とは，ことばを用いずに腹のうちを相手に伝えることをいう。"What the mind thinks, the heart transmits" の意味である。ほかの社会，とりわけ西洋では，理解を十分にはかるため，明確なことばで表現して，コミュニケートするのがふつうである。だから，西洋の人からみると，日本人は霊感をもっているのではないか，と思ったりする。ことばを用いずにコミュニケートできるからである。

This is because the many formalities, conventions and common standards developed in a society which gives priority to harmonious relations makes it easy to understand what goes on in the mind of the other person.

The younger generation of Japanese who have become more individualistic are losing the **ishin-denshin** faculty.

→ **Hara-gei**

Jihyõ

In Japan, because of the lifetime employment system, employees generally do not resign from a company. Resignation is usually regarded as a very grave matter. When a person wishes to quit a company, he must submit a **jihyõ** — a formal letter of resignation. An intent to resign transmitted verbally has no force and is completely disregarded.

It happens quite often that the management refuses to accept a **jihyõ**, although it has no legal power to prevent an employee from quitting. However, in the Japanese social climate which demands a harmonious solution to everything, it is socially difficult for the employee to quit his job unless the management agrees to let him go. If agreement is given, it becomes **en·man-taisha** — leaving a company in an amicable manner.

ことばをつかわずに分かりあえるのは，日本の社会の定まりごと，しきたり，共通の基準といったものが，事を荒立てぬをもって旨としているので，相手の心の内の動きを読めるからである。日本人でも，若い世代は，だんだんと個人主義的になってきたので「以心伝心」の霊感を失いつつあるようだ。

　→ 腹芸

辞表

　日本は終身雇用制である。だから，一般に会社員が自分から辞めることはない。辞職はよほどの重大事，というのが通念になっている。会社を辞めたいときは，「辞表」（ a formal letter of resignation ）を提出せねばならない。口頭で辞意を伝えても効力はないし，まったく無視されてしまう。

　会社側が辞表を受理しないこともよくある。従業員がやめるのを阻止する権限などなにもないのに，である。しかし，日本の社会風土では，万事まるく納めるのがしきたりだから，会社側の同意がないのに辞めるのは，辞めた本人にとって不利となる。承諾があれば「円満退社」（ leaving a company in an amicable manner ）ということになる。

Jinji-idõ

March is a month of anxious expectation for workers in the Japanese corporate world because most companies and government offices carry out their annual large-scale staff reassignments (**jinji-idõ**) before the new fiscal year starts in April. (Minor changes are made around October also.)

Periodic job rotation of personnel at all levels is a common practice in Japan. It is a system for developing human resources — a versatile staff capable of undertaking a wide variety of tasks and a managerial class which has a company-wide outlook.

At the middle management level, certain posts are considered as stepping stones to executive positions. Thus, under the Japanese seniority system, persons who reach an age which qualifies them for such key posts become particularly anxious because the next **jinji-idõ** may determine the rest of their career in the company. **Jinji-idõ** is an important event for outsiders, too, because it directly affects their contacts in the company.

Jin-myaku

This is a newly coined word which is not found in dictionaries but is widely used in all walks of life because it aptly expresses one of

人事異動

　3月は，日本の会社に働く人にとって，不安と期待の交錯する月である。会社も官庁も，4月の新年度を機会に，年に1度の大規模な「人事異動」（staff reassignment ）を行なうからである（小異動が10月ごろにある）。どのレベルでも，定期的に仕事が変わるのは，日本では通例である。これは人的能力を開発する仕組みである。いろいろな仕事をなんでもこなし，全社的な視野から物がみられる管理職の人材を育成しよう，というものである。

　中間管理職には，重役への階段と目されるポストがいくつかある。したがって，年功序列制の日本では，重要なポストにそろそろ就いてもいい年齢に達した人は，とりわけ気がもめる。次の人事異動次第で，これからどこまで昇進できるかが決まってしまうからだ。人事異動は，社外の人にも重要である。その会社とのつながりに直接影響が出てくるからである。

人脈

　新語で，和英辞典にはのっていないが，あらゆる仕事の分野で広く使われている。仕事をする上で重要な要因をう

the vital factors of Japanese life. **Jin** means "man, person, human being", **myaku** means "vein" as in a vein of mineral deposits. The closest English equivalent is "personal connections".

The Japanese are cool towards people they don't know. But it is easy to thaw any Japanese if you know his **jin-myaku**. An introduction from anyone in his **jin-myaku** works like magic, swiftly and easily opening doors which reason, persuasion or argument could not pry open.

The building up of **jin-myaku** is a lifetime process, beginning in one's school days. A large **jin-myaku** is probably the biggest asset of the Japanese businessman, because human relationships are of paramount importance in Japanese society.

→ **Dōki, Batsu**

Jirei

Jirei is a piece of paper that brings joy or dismay to Japanese working in companies or government offices. Usually just a couple of lines on a single sheet of paper, the **jirei** notifies an individual that he has been employed, promoted, demoted, transferred, reassigned, dismissed or retired. The wording is usually expressed as an order. No personnel changes are carried out without a **jirei**.

まく表現したことばである。「人」は man, person, human being の意。「脈」は "vein" as in a vein of mineral deposits（鉱脈のようにつかわれる）。一番近い英語は "personal connection" である。

　日本人は，知らない人には冷淡に対応する傾向がある。しかし，人脈を知っていれば，打ち解けやすい。その人の人脈につながる筋の紹介があれば，理屈や説得，議論ではどうにもならぬ門でも，まるで魔法のように，たちどころにあっさりと開くのである。

　人脈を築くことは，学校時代から始まって，一生の仕事である。人脈が広いことは，日本のビジネスマンにとっては最大の資産になる。日本の社会では，人間関係がなによりも重要だからである。

　→同期，閥

辞令

　「辞令」は，会社や官庁に働く日本人にとって，哀歓をわける一片の紙である。ふつう「辞令」は1枚の紙にわずか2，3行で書かれた採用，昇進，降等，異動，配転，解雇，退職などの伝達書である。一般に，その語調は命令調で，これなしに人事異動は行なわれない。

Spring is the season of the **jirei** because it is the time when recruits fresh out of college are employed en masse and organizations carry out a wholesale reshuffle of assignments. Once a **jirei** is issued there is no chance of it being withdrawn.

There is, however, one type of **jirei** which is not final. It is the **shimbun** (newspaper) **jirei**, the name given cynically to newspaper reports of pending appointments of top-level personnel.

→ **Jinji-ido**

Kabu ga agaru

This expression has the same meaning as the English "his stock rises" and is used in exactly the same way. Employed as a metaphor, it means one's stock rises or one's public esteem goes up, or one gains in stature. The reverse is **kabu ga sagaru** or "his stock falls".

In Japanese society, where human relations and reputation among one's fellows are of the utmost importance, these two terms are heard very often and can have far-reaching consequences for the persons so described. Thus, there is a doomsday sound to **kabu ga sagaru**.

Kachō, Kasei

The organization of a Japanese business corporation is generally division-department-section. In most cases, the section is known as **ka**. Literally translated, **kasei** means "section system".

春は辞令の季節である。大学を出たばかりの新人が大量に採用されるし，組織全体が大幅な異動を行なう時期だからだ。いったん辞令が出てしまうと，撤回されることはない。辞令には，本決まりでないものもある。これを「新聞（newspaper）辞令」という。新聞がトップ・レベルの人事を未決定のうちに報道してしまうのを皮肉ったいい方である。

　　→ 人事異動

株が上がる

　これは英語でいう "his stock rises" と同じ意味である。比喩に使うときは "one's stock rises" とか "one's public esteem goes up" とか "one gains in stature" の意味になる。反対に，「株が下がる」とは "his stock falls" である。

　人間関係と仲間うちの評判がなによりも大事な日本の社会では，この両方のいい方が実によく聞かれる。そういわれた人は重大な影響を受ける。「株が下がる」には，"この世の終わり" のような響きがある。

課長，課制

　日本の会社組織は，一般に部課制をとっている。通常，section は「課」である。「課制」は section system。日常

Kasei is also used to refer to the fact that the **ka** is the level at which all routine business is dispatched. The section manager, known as **kachõ**, therefore, holds an important position in the middle management of Japanese firms. He is the key man, around 40 years in age, who makes all the routine business decisions and supervises the implementation of those decisions. Special project teams and groups are also usually organized at the level of **ka**.

A word of warning: in the Ministry of International Trade and Industry, the majority of **ka** are known in English as "division" and a few as "section".

→ **Buchõ**

Kaigi

Some students of the Japanese style of management say that consensus formation takes the place of the process which in other countries is known as decision making. **Kaigi** is a meeting or conference held to discuss problems and eventually to reach a consensus.

The meeting may be of members of the same department or of representatives of several departments. **Kaigi** is also a meeting with representatives of outside organizations. Some Japanese executives complain that there are too many **kaigi** in their business life; they believe that intra-office telephone calls, memos and the distribution of

業務を処理するレベルを指すとき課制という。だから，section manager つまり「課長」は，日本では中間管理職として重要なポストにあるわけだ。年齢も40歳前後の働き盛り。日常業務をとりしきり，決定事項を監督するカナメの存在である。特別のプロジェクト・チームやグループも課レベルで組織される。

　注意：通産省（MITI）では，ほとんどの課が division と呼ばれているが，まれには section と呼ばれているものもある。

　→部長

会議

　日本式経営を研究している人達がよくいうが，日本では，他の国での意思決定プロセスにかわるものが，コンセンサス作りである。会議は，問題を討議し，最終的にコンセンサスに達するための a meeting または conference である。

　会議に出るのは，同じ部課の人，またはいくつかの部課の代表である。会議には他社の代表との meeting もある。日本の重役は，会議が多すぎて，ろくに仕事もできない，

reports could take the place of many of the meetings.

A foreign businessman calling on a Japanese executive to discuss some matter informally is already in **kaigi** with his counterpart's colleagues and aides even if the foreigner does not realize it, because the matter will be brought up at an intra-office **kaigi** afterwards.

Kaki-ire-doki

Every year shops and department stores in Japan have two **kaki-ire-doki** —— the traditional gift-giving seasons in midsummer and December. This is a term used to mean "the season when earnings are big" or "raking-in time".

Literally translated the Chinese characters mean "time to write in". Some dictionaries explain the meaning as "the period when merchants are kept busy writing their sales into the ledger". The origin of the word, however, is not so cheerful. Originally it meant "put up as security" and came from writing in (**kaki-ire**) on an I.O.U. the item put up as collateral for a loan.

Over the years, the way the term was used underwent changes and eventually assumed its current meaning. The term, of course, is not limited to describing the rush season for retail-

とこぼす。電話ですませたり報告を回せば，会議を開くには及ばない，と思っている人もいる。

外国のビジネスマンが，ある問題を内々に話しあうため，日本の重役を訪問するとき，たとえ，その人には気付かれなくとも，すでに予備会議にかけられている。その問題が，あとであらためて会議にかけられるからである。

書き入れ時

日本の商店やデパートでは，「書き入れ時」が年に2回ある。夏のなかばと12月で，しきたりで贈物をする季節でもある。「書き入れ時」は "the season when earnings are big"（水あげが増える時期）とか "raking-in time" の意味につかわれる。

直訳すると，time to write in である。辞書によっては「商人が売上げを元帳に書き込むのに忙しい時期」とある。しかし，元の意味は，そんなに景気のいいものではない。もとは「担保として出す」の意味で，貸付けの担保として，借用証に書き入れることからきている。

それが，いつしか使い方が変わってきて，いまのような意味になった。もちろん，このことばは，小売商の忙しい

ers. Other kinds of business may have their own **kaki-ire-doki**.

→ **Nippachi**

Kaki-kyũka

Kaki-kyũka means summer vacation. Although still not on the scale of European countries, **kaki-kyũka** has become in recent years an established institution for corporate employees in Japan, too. It has become customary for an entire factory to shut down for a week or so during the hottest period, while the office staff adjust their schedules to take their vacation alternately. Many companies even urge their employees to take part of their annual leave during July and August in addition to the special **kaki-kyũka**.

The businessman uses the summer vacation as a time to make his family happy, with a visit to seaside or mountain resorts to escape from the oppressive heat and humidity of the Japanese summer.

→ **Yũkyũ-kyũka**

Kakushi-gei

Japanese businessmen are all expected to have a **kakushi-gei**, literally, a hidden talent. The talent referred to, however, has nothing directly to do with business or managerial ability. It refers to

時期を指すだけとはかぎらない。他の商売にも，それぞれ
に書き入れ時がある。

→ 二八

夏季休暇

「夏季休暇」とは summer vacation のこと。欧米並み
とまではいかないが，日本でも近年は夏季休暇が定着して
きた。夏の暑い盛りに，工場全体が1週間くらい閉まるの
は，当たり前になってきた。事務職も予定をやりくりして
交代で休暇をとる。年次休暇も夏季休暇に加えて，7月と
8月にとるよう勧めている会社も多い。会社員は夏休みに
海や山に出かけて，家族を楽しませ，日本のむし暑い夏を
しのごうとする。

→ 有給休暇

かくし芸

日本の会社員は，だれでも「かくし芸」をもっているの
が当たり前のように思われている。直訳すると hidden talent である。しかし，この場合の才能は，仕事や管理能力
に直接の関係はない。歌ったり，楽器を奏でたり，詩吟を

singing, playing a musical instrument, reciting, mimicking, parlor stunt, magician's trick or any such amateur entertaining ability.

At office parties, every person attending is called upon to display his **kakushi-gei**. On such an occasion, if you really have a hidden talent which nobody knew about, you create a good impression. Those who don't have any, usually sing a currently popular song or a tune which they learned long ago. This custom of everybody contributing to the entertainment helps not only to liven up a party but also to build up camaraderie.

When parties are given for clients, some really talented persons on the host's side are called upon to demonstrate their **kakushi-gei**. Not a few corporate employees spend some of their free time polishing a performance expressly for use at parties.

→ **Ohako, Kangei-kai, Bõnen-kai**

Kangaete okimasu

If the Japanese you are negotiating with tells you in English "I'll think it over" or "I'll give it a thought", don't go away feeling that you might get a favorable answer. Like as not, what the Japanese said was a literal translation of

したり，物まねをしたり，曲芸をみせたり，手品をしたり，といった素人芸ができることをいう。

会社の宴席では，出席者はひとり残らずかくし芸の披露をせがまれる。そのとき，人の知らないかくし芸をもっていれば，一同は感心してしまう。なにもなければ，いまはやりの歌を歌ったり，昔おぼえた歌をうたったりする。皆が即興に一枚加わるというしきたりは，宴席を盛り上げるばかりか，仲間意識を深めるのに役立つ。お客を招いた席では，招待側から芸達者が指名されてかくし芸を披露する。宴席の芸をなにかひとつ，休みのときに練習する会社員も多い。

→ おはこ，歓迎会，忘年会

考えておきます

交渉相手の日本人が "I'll think it over" とか "I'll give it a thought" といったからとて，OKの返事がもらえるかもしれない，などと期待してはいけない。多分，その日本人は，日本語の「考えておきます」をそのまま英

kangaete okimasu and he probably believed that he conveyed to you the nuance contained in the Japanese expression.

When a Japanese hears **kangaete okimasu**, he generally concludes that it is hopeless, because in the unwritten rules of social communication in Japan, it is a polite way of saying "no". Conversely, if you tell a Japanese "I'll think it over," he might take it that you mean **kangaete okimasu** and that he has been refused.

If both sides were familiar with the difference between **kangaete okimasu** and "I'll think it over", there would be less chance of misunderstanding.

→ **Zensho shimasu**

Kangei-kai and Sõbetsu-kai

The frequent holding of **kangei-kai** (welcoming party) by businessmen as well as by people in other walks of life, is one of the ways in which the Japanese exhibit their "groupism".

When new recruits join a company, a **kangei-kai** is held to welcome them. When a person is assigned to a new department, he is welcomed with a **kangei-kai**. When a staff member returns from an overseas assignment, he also is given a **kangei-kai**. **Sake** flows at the **kangei-kai** and the atmosphere is relaxed. The **kangei-kai** plays a very important role in Japanese society because it helps strengthen the newcomer's (or returnee's)

語に訳したのであり，それで日本語の表現の含蓄を相手に伝えたと思い込んでいるのだ。

日本人ならふつう，「考えておきます」といわれると，これは望みがないな，と判断する。日本の社会的コミュニケーションの不文律により，丁重な言い回しで no といったことになるのである。逆に，あなたが，日本人に向かって "I'll think it over" というと，相手は「考えておきます」の意味にとり，断られたと解釈する。

双方ともに，「考えておきます」と "I'll think it over" の違い，ニュアンスの差がよく分かっていれば，誤解は少なくなる。

→ 善処します

歓迎会と送別会

ビジネスマンも他の職業の人も，よく「歓迎会」（ welcoming party ）を開く。日本人の集団主義のあらわれのひとつである。新人が入社すると歓迎会を開く。新しい部課に配属されると歓迎会で迎えられる。海外勤務から帰任したときも歓迎会がある。歓迎会では酒が汲み交わされ，雰囲気がぐっと砕ける。歓迎会は日本の社会でとても重要な役割を果たす。新人または帰国者の所属意識を深め，集団精神を高め，団結を強め，一体感を密にする。

歓迎会の逆が「送別会」（ farewell or send-off party）である。出てゆく人のポストに代わりの人が新たにくるときは，歓迎会と送別会をひとまとめにして「歓送迎会」をするのがふつうである。

→ 忘年会

feeling of belonging, enhances group spirit, pro-
motes solidarity, and develops a sense of identity.

The opposite of the welcoming party is the
sõbetsu-kai (farewell or send-off party) which
usually turns out to be rather emotional. When
a newcomer comes to take the place of a de-
parting member, it is customary to combine the
two parties into a single **kansõgei-kai**.

→ **Bõnen-kai**

Kao

Kao (face) can be a vital factor in conducting
business in any country. The great importance
which the Japanese place on it is seen from the
many expressions in the language which use **kao**.

First among these is, of course, **kao wo tateru**
(to give face or to save face). Extended meanings
of this can be "for your sake" and "to prevent
one from disgrace or dishonor". Because consideration for the other party's honor and reputation
is so important in Japanese human relations, this
expression is heard all the time. The opposite of
give one face is **kao wo tsubusu** (to cause a loss of
face).

In doing business, it is an advantage to be a

顔

　「顔」（ face ）は，国の如何を問わず，商売にはきわめて
重要である。日本人が顔を重んじることは，顔を使った表
現がたくさんあることでもわかる。

　その第1は，なんといっても「顔を立てる」(to　give
face とか to save face ）である。これを拡大して for
your sake（あなたのために）とか to prevent one from
disgrace or dishonor（不名誉なことにならないように）
という意味になる。相手の名誉や評判を損なわないよう気
を遣うことが，日本の人間関係ではとても大事なので，こ
のことばはよく聞かれる。顔を立てるの反対は「顔をつぶ
す」である。

　仕事をするには「顔が広い」(a person who has many

89

person whose **kao ga hiroi** — a person who has many contacts. A person who has many contacts is constantly doing things to **kao wo tsunagu** — keep up contacts already made. He might do so by casually dropping into the other person's office from time to time, inviting him to lunch or golf, sending gifts at the mid-summer and year-end gift-giving seasons, and never failing to send New Year's greetings.

Having many contacts with ordinary people isn't as useful as knowing persons whose **kao ga kiku**. These are people with influence whose word goes a long way.

The Japanese also say **kao wo uru**, whose direct translation, "to sell face" tells you at once that it means "to sell or advertise oneself".

The face can also be "loaned", as in the expression **kao wo kasu**. "Lend me your face" (**kao wo kase**) would mean "I want to have a talk with you".

Many of the expressions that deal with the face are regarded as underworld lingo. **Kao wo uru** and **kao wo kasu**, in particular, have a strong underworld tone.

Kata-tataki

Kata-tataki is a word dreaded by government employees who are past the age of 55 or so. The term simply means "tap on the shoulder", but in

contacts）と都合がいい。たくさんの "コネ" があり，顔が広い人は，「顔をつなぐ」(keep up contacts already made ）ことに平常からつとめている。知人のオフィスにときどきぶらりと立ち寄る，昼めしやゴルフに誘う，盆暮れには付け届をする，年賀状を欠かさないなど。

普通の人との "コネ" をいくらたくさんもっていても，「顔のきく人」を知っていることには敵わない。顔のきく人とはそのことばに千金の重みがある実力者のことである。

「顔を売る」というのもある。直訳して sell the face といった方が，自分を売り込む(sell oneself, advertise oneself ）のことだな，とすぐわかる。

顔は貸す（ loan ）こともできる。「ちょっと顔を貸せ」(Lend me your face ）といえば，「話したいことがある」(I want to have a talk with you.) といった意味である。

ただし顔に関するいいまわしは，たくさんあるが，多くは，"やくざ" の陰語とみなされている。「顔を売る」「顔を貸す」などは，特にこの意味あいが強い。

肩たたき

「肩たたき」と聞くと，55歳を過ぎた官公庁の職員は，ぞっとする。英語では，"tap on the shoulder" というだけの

the civil service it has an ominous ring. A worker is approached gently by his superior — an actual physical tap on the shoulder may not take place — with a hint that it's about time he retired from the service.

In the civil service, there is no fixed compulsory retirement age. Unless a worker retires of his own will, the government cannot fire him. Thus, there are cases of workers staying on even past 70. It is for this reason that the **kata-tataki** form is employed when a government department feels that the usefulness of a worker has ended because of his advanced age.

A few people resist, but in general most government employees take the hint, because if they do, they will be promoted one rank and receive a larger retirement allowance and pension.

→ **Kibõ-taishoku**

Katte-deru

Katte-deru is a colorful expression essentially meaning "to volunteer". But often, it conveys a nuance that goes beyond simple volunteering. For instance, it is often used to mean "to undertake a task or challenge which others shun, although one was not asked to do so and although it is not really one's business".

The expression literally means "pay to enter the fray," and it originated as a gambling term.

ことだが，実は，公務員の間では不吉な響きをもつ。上役がやさしい物腰で近付いてくる——実際に肩をたたくことはないかもしれないが，もうそろそろ勇退してもいい頃合いではないか，といわんばかりに，やんわりとくる。公務員に定年はない。自由意思で辞めないかぎり，官庁側は解雇するわけにはいかない。だから，70歳を過ぎても，まだ頑張っているケースがある。そこで，官庁側が，あの人も歳のせいでもう役に立たなくなった，と判断したときに，肩たたき方式がとられる。首をタテに振らない人もなかにはいるが，大体は察しをつけて辞める。その方が，1号俸上がり，したがって退職金と年金がそれだけふえるからだ。

→ 希望退職

買って出る

「買って出る」とは，もともと to volunteer のことだが，いろいろな含みがある。進んで申し出るだけでなく，それ以上のニュアンスをもつばあいが多い。たとえば，「ほかの人ならいやがる仕事や難問に，頼まれもしないのに，また自分にかかわりあいのないことなのに，引き受ける」といった意味である。直訳すると "pay to enter the fray" で，賭博からきたことばである。人数に制限のあるポーカー・

In a card game in which the number of players was limited, a latecomer had to pay money to someone already seated at the table to buy a seat so that he could enter the game. From this, **katte-deru** came to mean "getting into the act voluntarily from the sidelines".

Kekkõ desu

You will hear this phrase spoken very often at the dinner table. But, watch out. It can mean "This tastes good," or "No thanks, I've had enough," or "That's a good idea. I'll have another helping". Which of these three is meant depends on the situation, the speaker's intonation and sometimes the linkage with other words.

Because of its three meanings, it lends itself to some good-natured fun. The hostess asks, "Won't you have some more?" The guest answers, **kekkõ desu**, meaning that he has had enough. The hostess shoots back, "If you think it's **kekkõ**, (meaning 'splendid'), you must have some more".

ゲームのばあい，あとからこれに参加するには，先にテーブルについている人にお金を払ってその席を買わねばならなかった。ここから買って出るとは "getting into the act voluntarily from the sidelines" という意味になった。

結構です

食事の席でよく耳にすることばである。しかし，要注意。その意味には「おいしい」もあれば「いや，いりません。十分に頂戴しました」もあれば，「はい，お代わりを頂きましょう」もある。この３つのうち，どの意味をさすのかは，そのときの状況，話す人のいい回し，前後のことばの関連で決まってくる。

意味に３つあることから，こんな軽い冗談も生まれる。招待した家の奥さんが「もう少しいかがですか」と勧める。お客は答える。「結構です。」もう十分ごちそうになった，という意味である。それを承知のうえで奥さんが切り返す。「結構 (delicious) でしたら，もっとお上がり下さらなくっちゃ。」

食事の席でつかうだけではない。どんなときでも次の３

But it's not just a dinner table word. In any situation, it can be used in its three meanings of "good, fine, etc.", "I've had enough, I'm satisfied" or "with pleasure".

Ki

Ki is a versatile word whose meanings include spirit, mind, heart, will, intention, feelings, mood, nature and disposition —— the abstract qualities which concern the heart and mind. It can also mean care, precaution, attention, air, atmosphere, flavor, and smell. Expressions given here are those which relate to the first group of meanings.

A very popular expression is **ki wa kokoro** ("**ki** is heart") which means that the gesture may be small but it shows sincerity or goodwill or genuine gratitude or desire to help.

If you feel **ki ni kuwanai** about the performance of your subordinate, you think it is unsatisfactory or you are displeased with it. If you feel your boss is a **ki ni kuwanai** person, it means you think he is a disagreeable fellow. (→ **hada ni awanai**) The opposite is **ki ni iru** —— to like, to find agreeable, to suit one's taste, etc.

When a person "pulls out the **ki**" (**ki wo nuku**) it means he has become unenthusiastic, lukewarm, discouraged, dispirited, careless. When "**ki** does not go into" (**ki ga hairanu**) any endeavor or undertaking, it means one cannot become enthu-

つの意味でつかってよい。「よい」（good）とか「立派」（fine），「十分に頂いたので満足している」（I've had enough, I'm satisfied），それに「喜んで」（with pleasure）である。

気

「気」はいろいろにつかわれる。権威ある辞典によると，spirit（精神），mind（心），heart（気持ち），will（決意），intention（意思），feeling（感情），mood（気分），nature（性質），disposition（性癖），care（注意），precaution（用心），flavor（香），smell（匂），とある。つかい方で意味も違ってくる。

一番よく使われるのが「気は心」（"Ki is heart."）。意味は，形にあらわれたものがささやかであっても，内に誠意とか心からの感謝，助けたい気持ちなどがこもっていること。部下の仕事振りが「気に食わない」とは，unsatisfactory（不満）だったり，displease（不機嫌）であること（「肌に合わない」参照）。この反対は「気に入る」to like, to find agreeable, to suit one's taste である。

「気を抜く」（pull out the ki）とは，unenthusiastic（身を入れない），lukewarm（気乗りしない），discouraged（意欲を失っている），dispirited（元気のない），careless（不注意な）こと。事をやるのに「気が入らぬ」（ki does not go into）とは，熱が入らない（cannot become enthusiastic about it.

Ki can also be rubbed or massaged — **ki wo momu**. In this case, a person is worried or anxious about something and becomes nervous and fidgety. **Ki wo momaseru** is to keep a person in suspense or on tenterhooks.

Ki wo hiku (draw the **ki**) is to sound out the intentions of the other party.

Kinori usu (the **ki** is thin) means lackluster, lethargic, stagnant or unenthusiastic, and can be used to describe the performance of the stock market.

Kibõ-taishoku

Under Japan's lifetime employment system, all corporations have a compulsory retirement age which at present generally ranges between 55 and 60. The retiring employee automatically receives a retirement allowance calculated according to a ratio indexed to his length of service and basic salary. In the event an employee resigns for personal reasons before his automatic retirement age, the allowance will be reduced considerably below the standard.

When the big jump in oil prices reduced corporate earnings, many companies adopted the policy of "weight-reducing" to cut down overhead. Instead of dismissing, say 100 employees outright, the company asked for voluntary resignations of 100 employees, offering as an inducement allowances considerably more than the

siastic）のこと。

Ki は，rub や massage することもできる——「気を揉む」である。このばあいは，なにかにくよくよ心配したり（worried, anxious），神経質になったり（nervous），落ちつかない（fidgety）こと。「気を揉ませる」は，人を suspense や tenterhook（宙ぶらりん）の状態におくこと。

「気を引く」は，相手の意向を探ること。

株の用語に「気乗り薄」（ki-ride-thin）がある。市況が lackluster（活気がない），lethargic（低調），stagnant（低迷）の意。

希望退職

日本は終身雇用制であり，どの会社にも定年がある。いまは，大体55歳から60歳の間である。退職者には自動的に退職金が支給される。勤続年数と基本給を基準に一定の割合を掛けた額である。定年まえに個人的な理由で退職するばあい，退職金は標準よりずっと少なくなる。

石油価格の急騰で，会社が減益になったため，経費切詰めの "減量" 政策をとるところが多かった。たとえば，100人をすっぱり解雇する代わりに，標準額よりもかなりの色

standard sum. Employees who took advantage of this offer were treated as **kibõ-taishoku**, literally, leaving the company of their own wish, but different from resigning for personal reasons, or **jiko-taishoku**.

→ **Jihyõ, Kata-tataki**

Kogai

Originally **kogai** meant a pet, like a dog or cat, which one brought up from a puppy or a kitten, or the act of doing so.

The word later came to be used to refer to a person who apprenticed himself as a child to work under a merchant or artisan under the old teacher-disciple system. Today, a person who receives the favors and patronage of a superior under whom he has served since joining the company is called the **kogai** of that superior. Such a person would be a devoted and trusted subordinate.

The contrasting word is **tozama**. The word which originally was the opposite of **tozama** was **fudai** which referred to a hereditary vassal or successive generations of the same family serving under the same feudal lord's family. This latter word is not used so much in today's business society because it is rare for successive generations of the same family to work in the same company, still less for father and son to be the subordinates

をつけて自発的退職を求める。この申し出に乗る人は、「希望退職」扱いとなる。自分の意思でやめることには変わりないのだが、個人的な理由による「自己退職」とは違う。

→ 辞表、肩たたき

子飼い

本来は、犬猫など、子どもから飼い育てるペット、またはそのような飼い方をいう。転じて少年のころから弟子として働く徒弟制度下の商人、職人のことを指す。現代では新入社員当時から一定の上司に仕え、可愛がられ、引き立てられているようなばあい「彼はA氏の子飼いだ」などという。信頼されている腹心の部下の意味になる。

対することばは「外様」だが、もともと外様と対比されることば「譜代」は、ビジネス社会ではあまり使われない。特定の領主家に代々仕えてきた家臣を譜代の臣と呼ぶのだが、現代では特定企業に代々勤めるなどは稀であり、まして特定の人に親子とも部下になることなどは無いからだろ

of the same boss.

→ **Tozama**

Konjõ

A businessman who is described as **konjõ ga aru** (possessing **konjõ**) is one who has "fighting spirit, will power, determination, tenacity and guts". He is a person who gets things done even against great odds. Adversity never gets him down. In fact, adversity spurs him on to greater efforts. He is a tough negotiator who never gives up. The opposite is **konjõ ga nai**.

To his boss, the **konjõ ga aru** subordinate is one who can be trusted to carry out the most difficult assignment without a word of complaint. The boss does not have to keep looking over his shoulder or give him pep talks. **Konjõ**, therefore is that extra element, aside from expertise or experience, which gives an added value to a businessman.

Kõsai-hi

In general **kõsai-hi** is money spent for main-

うか。

→ 外様

根性

あの人は「根性がある」といえば、「闘志，意思力，決意，辛抱強さ，度胸」のある人である。条件が悪いのに立派に事を成し遂げる人のことである。逆境にあって挫けない人のことである。それどころか，逆境に立つと，かえって勇気百倍する人である。交渉相手としては，タフである。絶対に諦めない。「根性がある」の反対は「根性がない」。

上司にとって根性がある部下は頼りになる。どんなにむずかしい仕事でも，文句ひとついわずにやってくれるからだ。肩ごしにいちいち点検したり，はっぱをかけたりする必要はない。だから，ビジネスマンにとって，「根性」は，専門知識とか経験とは別に，特別の資質であり，その人の値打ちを高めるものである。

交際費

一般に「交際費」とは，社交や友人の接待に支出する費

taining social contacts or entertaining friends. In the business world it is the entertainment expense account. Although business entertainment is a common practice in all parts of the world, it probably plays a bigger role in Japan than in other countries. This is because human relations are all-important in Japanese society and **sake** lubricates those relations better than anything else.

It is said that the majority of expensive bars and night-clubs in Tokyo would close overnight if the expense account system were abolished, because they are patronized almost wholly by people with fat expense accounts. Under today's depressed business conditions, more and more business entertainment is taking the form of a lunch instead of expensive dining and wining at night.

→ **Shayō-zoku**

Koshi

As the pivotal part of the body, the **koshi** (waist, hip, loin) appears in many expressions which describe things as being one way or the other.

For instance, we say **koshi ga hikui** (low) or **takai** (high). Low waist means humble, modest, unassuming, polite and conversely high waist means proud, haughty.

用をいう。ビジネスマンの世界では，饗応用の支出勘定をいう。商売上の接待は，世界共通の慣行だが，どこよりも一番大きな役割を果しているのは日本であろう。日本の社会では，人間関係がなによりも大切であり，酒はなにものにもまして人間関係を円滑にするからだ。

　東京で，目の飛び出るほど高いバーやナイトクラブは，交際費制度がなくなってしまったら，一夜にして店をたたまなければならなくなるであろう。それほど交際費をふんだんに使える人でもっているようなものである。いまは不景気なので，金のかかる夜の飲み食いから昼食の接待に変わりつつある。

　→ 社用族

腰

　「腰」（ waist, hip, loin ）は身体の大事な部分なので，これをつかった表現は多い。たとえば，「腰が低い」（low）とか「高い」（ high ）という。低いのは humble （謙遜），modest （穏やか）, unassuming （高ぶらない）, polite （丁寧な）こと。反対に「腰が高い」のは proud （高慢）とかhaughty （横柄）なこと。

A person whose **koshi ga karui** (light) is one who is quick to act, nimble, or willing to work. Conversely, the person whose waist is **omoi** (heavy) is one who is slow to act, unwilling to work or dilly-dallies. It is not advisable to say **koshi ga karui** of a woman because it can be taken to mean she flits from one man to another.

Koshi wo ageru is to raise the waist, which not only means that a person gets up physically from a sitting position but also describes a person who has just been watching the situation and has now decided to take action. (→ **Mikoshi**)

Koshi wo sueru is to let the waist settle down, which means settling down to a steady course of action or undertaking something seriously or with determination.

To do something with **oyobi-goshi** is to do it in an unsteady position, with bent back or leaning over. Thus, it is used to describe a person whose heart is not in his work.

Koshi-kudake is a person whose "waist breaks down" or a weak-kneed person. Coming from a **sumō** (Japanese wrestling) term meaning breaking down in the middle of a bout, it usually describes a person who falls apart at a crucial moment in, say, business negotiations.

When some event causes a person's "hip to become disjointed" (**koshi ga nukeru**), he is overwhelmed by the enormity of the thing or paralyzed with fear.

「腰が軽い」（light）といえば，"quik to act"（気軽に動き出す），nimble（すばしこい），または "willing to work"（積極的にやる）人のこと。逆に，「腰が重い」（heavy）とは，"slow to act"（なかなか動き出さない），"unwilling to work"（あまりやる気がない），または dilly-dallies（ぐずぐずする）人のこと。腰が軽いを女性には使わぬ方がよろしい。男の誘いに簡単に乗る尻軽女にとられるからだ。

「腰を上げる」は "to raise the waist"。座っている場所から立ち上がることだが，情勢を観望したのちに，やっと行動に移る決心を固めることにもいう。（→みこし）

「腰を据える」は "to let the waist settle down"。じっくりと着実に行動すること。真剣に，決意を固めて事に取り組むことをいう。

「及び腰で事をする」とは，腰をまげたり（bent back），前かがみ（leaning over）の不安定な姿勢で動作すること（to do it in an unsteady position）。本気で取り組む気持ちにない人を指す。

「腰くだけ」は "a person whose waist breaks down" とか "a weak-kneed person"（弱腰の人）。相撲からきたことばで，取り組みの最中に，受けこたえる腰の力がなくなって転がること。ここから商取引の大事な局面で，あとが続かずに潰れてしまうことをいう。

なにかの出来事で「腰が抜ける」（hip to become dis-jointed）とは，その物すごさに圧倒されて動けなくなること，恐怖でへなへなになってしまうこと。

Koshikake

By itself **koshikake** merely means a chair or a place to sit. But it is a word popularly used in Japanese companies in quite a different context.

How would you interpret it if you should hear a Japanese say, "I am in this company only as a **koshikake**?" Certainly, he couldn't mean that he is a chair. Or, "The vice president's post is a **koshikake** for Mr. Tanaka?" Or "Girl university graduates regard jobs in big corporations only as a **koshikake**?" Puzzling? Not if you substitute for **koshikake** in each question the concepts "a temporary position while looking for something better", "a position which is a stepping-stone to a higher post" and "a place to fill time before they get married".

In other words, the word is used to describe a post which is not regarded as permanent, but as a transit point.

Kubi

Japanese in responsible positions are fond of the expression **kubi wo kakete**, meaning "stake my neck", with the neck (**kubi**) being a reference to position, honor, reputation or even life. It is an expression of confidence and determination in undertaking some big task.

腰かけ

　「腰かけ」それ自体は chair であり，坐るところの意味である。だが，日本の会社ではまったく違った意味につかわれることがある。「ぼくは，この会社に腰かけでいるだけさ。」これをどう解釈するか。　自分が chair だ，というわけではない。あるいは「副社長のポストは田中さんには腰かけだ」とか，「大卒の女子は会社に勤めても腰かけぐらいにしか思っていない。」なんのことやら，さっぱりわからないって？　いずれの例も，腰かけを「もっといいポストを待っている間の一時的な地位」とか，「もっと上のポストに就く踏み台の地位」とか，「結婚するまでの間の時間つぶしのところ」といった風に置きかえれば，さらりと解ける。つまり，永続的なものでなく，一時のつなぎのポストを指すときにつかう。

首

　責任ある地位にいる人がよく「首をかけて」という。"stake my neck" のこと。この neck（首）は地位とか名誉，評判ないし生命そのものを指す。なにか大仕事に取り組むときに自信と決意のほどを示すことばである。

Of course in a Japanese corporation, it is pretty safe to "stake one's neck" because under the lifetime employment system it is rare that one's **kubi ga tobu** (to be fired). This is not to say that companies never carry out **kubi-kiri** (personnel reduction), because extreme business conditions sometimes do make it necessary to scale down a company's operations in order to survive.

When a company, or an individual for that matter, finds itself up to its neck in debt (**kubi ga mawaranai**, or "cannot turn the neck"), it has to **kubi wo hineru** (wring the neck = rack the brain, think hard) to devise ways to get out of its straitened circumstances.

A euphemistic Japanese expression which uses the word **kubi** is **mawata de kubi wo shimeru**. The latter part of this expression translates as "strangle the neck". **Mawata** is delicate silk floss which is pleasing to the skin. Strangling a person with floss means using a gentle or indirect way to throttle a person gradually. It is used to describe an operation for easing a person out by gradually making it impossible for him to stay.
→ **Tsume-bara**

Kuromaku

The first part of the ideogram for **kuromaku** is written with the Chinese character for "black" and the latter part with the character for "cur-

もちろん，日本の会社では首をかけたところで心配はいらない。終身雇用制だから，「首がとぶ」（ to be fired ）ことはまずない。終身雇用制でも，会社側が「首切り」（ personnel reduction ）を絶対にやらないわけではない。極度の営業不振になって，会社が生き残るには業務の縮小に追い詰められることもある。

　会社でも個人でも，借金に首までつかっているとき，つまり「首が回らない」（ cannot turn the neck ）とき，打開策はないかと「首をひねる」（ wring the neck, または rack the brain ＝頭をしぼる。think hard ＝一所懸命考える）。

　首をつかった婉曲ないい回しに「真綿で首をしめる」がある。首をしめるは "strangle the neck"，真綿は肌にやさしいくず絹（ silk floss ）。真綿で首をしめるとは，おだやかな方法，間接的なやり方で人の首を徐々に締めつけていくことをいう。だんだんと窮地に追いこんで，ついにはいられなくなるように仕向けることである。

　→ 詰め腹

黒幕

　「黒幕」の「黒」は black，「幕」は curtain。昔，舞台

tain". In the old days, it used to be the backdrop behind a stage. Today, when a person is called a **kuromaku**, it means he is an influential man behind the scenes, the wire-puller who is hidden from public view or who doesn't hold an official post.

Such characters abound in every society, mostly in politics and government. Sometimes, it has a sinister connotation. In business, they are not found in individual corporations but there might be a **kuromaku** who is influential in a particular industry as a whole.

→ Õgosho

Ma

The basic meaning of **ma** is space, interval, time. Branching out from these are the meanings of chance, luck, occasion.

Ma wo motasu is "to fill in time" under special circumstances. For instance, people are gathered at a business meeting or a party at which a certain

の背景幕としてつかわれたもの。現代では, 黒幕とは, 舞台裏にあって影響力をもっている人, 表から見えないところで操る人, 表向きのポストに就いてない人をいう。

この種の人物は, どの社会にもいる。とりわけ政界に多い。あまりいい意味に使われない場合もある。ビジネスの世界となると, 個々の会社にはいなくても, その業界全体をみたとき, 影響力のある黒幕がいることはある。

→ 大御所

間 (ま)

もとの意味は, space (あいだ), interval (間隔), time (時間) のこと。これから派生して chance (機会), luck (運), occasion (ころ合い) の意味にもなる。

「間をもたす」は, 特別の状況下にあって "fill in time" のこと。たとえば, 仕事上の会議とかパーティに人が集まっていて, なにかが行なわれる予定になっている。ところ

thing is planned to take place. But before the time for it comes, an unexpected time gap occurs. To keep people entertained or occupied so that interest does not flag is **ma wo motasu**.

Ma wo ireru is literally "put in time", but not in the English sense of "serve". Here **ma** means an intentional pause or interval of time before taking action because certain considerations make such a pause necessary or desirable or strategically effective.

Ma ga warui is "**ma** is bad", but the reference is not to time but to situation. It means embarrassing and sometimes even unlucky.

Ma ga nukeru is "**ma** slips out", meaning "not in tune with things" or "out of place". "**Ma**" is something that is necessary at a given time or on a given occasion. If that something should be out of line or tune with respect to time or quality or character, it becomes useless or **ma-nuke** (**ma** is missing). Thus, a **ma-nuke** person is stupid, silly, slow-witted, dumb. When you are exasperated with a person's bungling and want to shout at him that he is an idiot, this is the word to use.

Madogiwa-zoku

Madogiwa is "beside the window" and **zoku** is "tribe". In almost every big Japanese business corporation you will find the "window-side tribe". They are people of the middle-echelon manager

が，その時刻になるまえに，思いもかけぬ時間のあきができてしまった。そこで参会者をしらけさせないように，面白がらせたり，注意を引きつけておいて，時間かせぎをするのが「間をもたす」である。

「間を入れる」は直訳すると "put in time" だが，英語の "serve"（つとめる）の意味ではない。ここにいう「間」とは，行動をとるまえにわざと一息いれること，時間をおくこと（pause or interval of time）。物を考えるのに，そうした「間」が必要であったり，望ましかったり，戦略的に効果的であったりするからだ。

「間が悪い」は "ma is bad" である。この「間」は時間でなく，状態を指す。きまりが悪いこと。ときには運が悪いことをも意味する。

「間が抜ける」は "ma slips out" である。つまり "not in tune with things"（かみ合わない）とか，"out of place"（場違い）のこと。

これに関連して「間抜け」（without ma）ともいう。stupid（ばか），silly（愚か），slow-witted（のろま），dumb（とんま）な人のこと。人がへまをやって頭にくる。"Idiot" と怒鳴りつけたいときは「この間抜け！」といえばいい。

窓際族

「窓際」とは beside the window，「族」は tribe である。日本では，大きな会社になると，まずどこにでも "window-side tribe" がいる。中間管理職クラスで，ふ

class who usually have the title of manager or sub-manager but no functions and duties.

Although in their younger days they played a very active part in the company's business, their climb up the promotion ladder has stopped. Under the seniority system, in order to make way for younger people, they have been removed from active duty. Under the lifetime employment system, however, they cannot be dismissed. And, in view of their rank, they are given desks in the best place in the office — beside the window — where they sit waiting for their retirement age to come. Thus, **madogiwa-zoku** is a word with a pathetic ring.

Mai hõmu

The Japanese businessman is generally thought of as an eager beaver employee racing on the promotional track in the company. He drudges all day long, sacrificing the time which business-men in other countries use to spend with their family. He does not use up the annual holidays to which he is entitled, because he thinks he is so

つうは部長とか次長の肩書をもっていながら，実際にやる仕事のない人達をいう。

　若いころは，会社のために一所懸命尽くしたのに，昇進への階段をぱったり閉ざされてしまった人達である。年功序列制の下で，後進に道を譲るために現役の仕事をはずされる。しかし，終身雇用制なので，解雇するわけにはいかない。その格付けからいっても，オフィスの一番よい上席——窓際に机を与えられ，ここで定年を待つ。だから，「窓際族」は，うら哀しい響きがあることばである。

マイホーム

　日本の勤め人というと，会社の出世街道にのろうと，ひたすらに働く人間のように思われている。日がな1日，他の国なら家族団らんの時間なのにそれまで犠牲にして，ただあくせくと働く。有給休暇があるのに，とらない。自分がいないことには毎日の仕事がはかどらない，だからいつ

indispensable in the company's day-to-day operation that he must be at the office all the time.

A generation ago, the above description applied to almost all Japanese. But not everybody is a workaholic these days. More and more businessmen of the younger generation are having second thoughts about the traditional values. They value family life as much as or more than business career. Their numbers have increased so much that a word has been coined for such people — "**Mai-hõmu-shugisha**" (my-home-ist).

Mã-mã

"How's your business?" "**Mã-mã desu**." (Not so bad, not so good.) "How did you like the new French restaurant?" "Did you enjoy the movie last night?" The answer can be "**mã-mã**," meaning "so-so". The expression usually implies lukewarm approval rather than disapproval. Sometimes it is purely non-committal, masking a lack of opinion.

Sometimes it is used in an obviously positive context. "My business is **mã-mã**" could actually mean "quite good", but the speaker is trying to be modest.

When your Japanese friends ask for your impressions about Japan, **mã-mã** is not recommended as an answer, because you will be taking the risk of implying that you haven't really en-

も出社していなければ，と思いこむ。

　一世代まえの勤め人は，だれもがそんな風だった。ところが近頃は，皆が皆，働き中毒ということはなくなった。若い世代の勤め人は，これまでの価値観を考え直すようになっている。仕事と同じくらいに，いやそれ以上に，家庭生活も大事にするようになった。そうした人達がふえているところから生まれた新語が「マイホーム主義者」（my-home-ist）である。

まあまあ

　「景気はどうですか」「まあまあですなあ」（そう悪くもなく，さりとてそう良くもない，といったところ）。「こんどできたフランス料理のレストラン，どうだった？」「ゆうべの映画，面白かった？」答えはどれも「まあまあ」だ。"so-so" である。否定するほどではないが，気乗りのしない肯定といったところだ。

　ときには意見がないのを覆い隠すため，どっちつかずの態度をとるのにつかう。

　明らかに肯定的につかうときもある。「仕事はまあまあです」自分のことを指すときには，本当は「たいへんうまくいっている」のに，へりくだっているわけだ。

　日本人の友人から「日本の印象は？」と聞かれて，「まあまあ」と答えるのは，あまり感心しない。日本での経験を

joyed your experience in Japan.

Meishi

The calling (business) card is a must in social and particularly business contacts in Japan. When one meets somebody for the first time, the **meishi** is exchanged instead of shaking hands as in the West. Any businessman who cannot produce a **meishi** has one strike against him. Businessmen keep a file of the cards they collect, and this is invaluable when the time comes to send out Christmas or New Year greeting cards.

Many Japanese businessmen have bilingual **meishi** with name, position, company name, address and phone number in Japanese on one side and in English on the other. If foreign businessmen visiting Japan want to be re-membered, they should have their **meishi** printed in the same manner. In major hotel arcades, there is usually a shop which undertakes 24-hour printing of **meishi.**

Mikoshi

Mikoshi is the portable **shinto** shrine which a group of young men in **happi** coats carry (**katsugu**) around the local parish on their shoulders during the annual festival while shouting "Wasshoi! Wasshoi!" It's a lively show which attracts big crowds. The expression **mikoshi wo katsugu** is

よく思っていない意味にとられる危険がある。

名刺

「名刺」（calling card or name card）は，日本では，社交とくに仕事の接触には欠せない。初対面では，欧米のように握手をしないで，名刺を交換する。名刺を出せない人は，最初の印象を損なう。

ビジネスマンは，名刺のファイルを作っておく。クリスマスカードや年賀状を出す季節になると役に立つ。

日本のビジネスマンの名刺には，氏名，肩書，会社名，住所，電話番号が，片面ずつ日本語と英語で記されている。

訪日する外国のビジネスマンが末永く覚えておいてもらいたいと思ったら，日本式の名刺を作ることである。主なホテルのアーケードには，24時間で名刺を作ってくれる店がある。

みこし（御輿）

「みこし」は，はっぴ姿の若者が幾人か組んでかつぐ，持ち運びのできる小型の "神社" である。年に一度のお祭りに　わっしょい，わっしょい」の掛け声も勇ましく，皆でかつぎながら，町内を練り歩く。活気にあふれ，見物人も大勢集まってくる。選挙の立候補者を，グループを作っ

used when people form a group to support or promote someone, such as a candidate in an election.

A commonly used expression in which the word appears is **mikoshi wo ageru** which means "get up from one's seat" or "take one's leave" after staying a bit too long. When one sits down for a long talk, it is **mikoshi wo suete hanashi-komu**, which can also mean he is overstaying his welcome.

→ **Koshi wo ageru/sueru**

Mizu

Mizu is water, but when you hear the word **mizu-shōbai** (water business) do not jump to the conclusion that it is the business of selling water. The word is used to describe a business whose earnings are greatly influenced by its popularity among customers. Specifically it means establishments like night-clubs, restaurants and theaters.

Figurative expressions using **mizu** are mostly easy to understand. **Mizu wo sasu** (to pour water) can readily be imagined as meaning "to pour cold water on" or "to put a damper on". The expression describes the act of a person who says or does a thing to put a brake on or foul up something that is proceeding smoothly. It is also used to mean "discourage a person" from carrying on with what he has been doing. Another sense in which the expression is used is "to alienate one

て支援したり，応援したりするのも「みこしをかつぐ」である。

　よく使われるいい方に「みこしを上げる」がある。「坐っている場所から腰を上げる」だが，長居してから帰る（take one's leave）意味である。どっかりと坐りこんで長談議するとき，「みこしを据えて話し込む」という。長尻も過ぎると，いい顔をされない。

　→腰を上げる / 据える

水

　「水」は water。そこで「水商売」（water business）と聞いて，水を売る商売だ，などと早とちりしてはいけない。収入が客の人気によって決まる不安定な商売のこと。とりわけ，ナイトクラブ，レストラン，映画・演劇のような店をいう。

　水を比喩的につかったことばは，分かりやすい。「水をさす」（to pour water）といえば，"to pour cold water on" とか，"to put a damper on"（勢いをくじく）ことだと，すぐ察しがつく。順調に進んでいることにブレーキをかけたり（brake on），混乱させる（foul up）ようなことをいったり，したりする行為が「水をさす」である。せっかく熱をこめてやっているのに，その人の気をそぐ（discourage）こともいう。人を仲違いさせる（to alienate one person from another）意味にも使う。

person from another".

Mizu-kake-ron (a water dousing argument) is an argument or discussion which reaches no conclusion. It's like the argument over which came first, the chicken or the egg. After a confrontation, the Japanese usually **mizu ni nagasu** (flush the water) which means "wash out the past" or "let bygones be bygones".

An often-used saying is **gaden-insui** which is literally "to draw water into (one's) paddy field". It describes the act of using given facts to one's own advantage in a debate or to take advantage of something to justify one's standpoint.

Mizuhiki torihiki means engineering a transaction by first taking a small loss in order to obtain a bigger profit later.

Yobi-mizu is "calling water" = priming water. It means something which serves as a lead to something else.

Naishoku

In the feudal days, **naishoku** meant the side-job of a **samurai** or the work done by **rōnin**. Today, it generally means the manual piecework which a housewife does at home. The number of housewives who work outside the home in part-time jobs or as cosmetics and life insurance saleswomen has increased recently, but this type of work is not called **naishoku.** Such work is known

「水掛け論」(water dousing argument) とは，結論の出ない議論や討議のこと。卵が先か鶏が先か，といった類の議論をいう。もめごとが終わると，日本人は「水に流す」(flush the water)。過ぎたことをさっぱり洗い落とす (wash out the past) とか，過去を水に流して，もうなかったことにする (let bygones be bygones) の意。

よく「我田引水」という。直訳は "to draw water into (one's) paddy field" (自分の田に水を引く)意から，ある事柄を自分に有利になるよう利用したり，自分の見解の正しさを示すためにうまく利用することをいう。

「水引き取引」とは，将来の大きな利益を期待して，目先では損をしても行なう取引のことである。

「呼び水」は，calling water ＝ priming water。 井戸に水を注入し，水が出るようにすること。すなわちものごとのきっかけを作ることをいう。

内職

古くは武士の副職，浪人の仕事として行なわれたものを指したが，現在では，一般に主婦が家内で行なう手作業的賃仕事を指すようになった。もっとも最近では主婦がパート・タイマーや化粧品のセールスマン，保険外交員など家庭外に出て働くことが多くなったが，これはアルバイトと呼ばれ，内職とはいわない。また主婦が結婚以前から，あ

as **arubaito.** When a housewife holds down a permanent job it is known as either **tomo-bataraki** (working together) or **tomo-kasegi** (earning together), assuming of course that her husband, too, is working. **Naishoku,** it seems, is the word reserved for work done at home for money.

When a corporate employee takes home work from the office, he might say jokingly, "I am going to do **naishoku** tonight", although he will not receive payment for it. These days, some people use their week-ends to write a novel at home, an act which falls under **naishoku.** But if, say, carpentering is your hobby, you would not describe it as doing **naishoku.** You are a Sunday carpenter or a Sunday artist, as the case may be.

→ **Arubaito**

Negai, Todoke

Negai, meaning request, and **todoke**, meaning report, are forms of paper work which keep the administrative machinery in large Japanese companies flowing smoothly.

Prescribed **negai** and **todoke** forms have to be filled in for routine matters such as requests for leave (annual, sick, maternity, etc.), office supplies and various payments, as well as reports on change of employee's address, family composition (births, deaths, etc.), minor changes in the work system, and so on.

るいは結婚後でも恒常的に仕事をもっているばあいは共働きとか共稼ぎといって区別する。あくまで家内で行なう仕事が内職と呼ばれる。

会社の仕事を一部家にもって帰って片付けるばあいも別に手当がもらえるわけではないが「今晩内職するよ」と冗談でいったりすることもある。近頃，週末を利用して小説を書いたりする人も多いが，これは内職のひとつである。── ただし趣味的なものは日曜大工とか日曜画家といって，内職に大工をしているとはいわない。

→アルバイト

願い，届け

「願い」は request，「届け」は report である。この書式がないと，大きな会社は順調に機能しない。

願いと届けは，あらかじめ書式ができていて，日常きまりきった事項について，書き込めばよいだけになっている。願いには，休暇願い（年次休暇，病気欠勤，出産休暇など）や事務用品請求の願いなど。届けには，住所変更届け，家族異動届け（出産，死亡など），作業変更届けなどがある。

The **negai** and **todoke** systems also are used in submitting requests and reports or notification to government offices, concerning both business and private matters. The paper work sometimes may seem troublesome but it is considered essential to administrative efficiency.

→ **Jihyõ**

Nemawashi

Literally, **nemawashi** means "to dig around the root of a tree to prepare it for transplanting". Adopted from this, the word refers to the groundwork to enlist support or to secure informal consent from the people concerned prior to a formal decision.

Japanese society operates on group decision or consensus, and **nemawashi** is an indispensable process in achieving consensus. It also avoids

仕事上ないし個人的な事柄について，官公庁に要請やら報告もしくは通告するときにも，書式による願いや届けを提出する。書類を書くことは，面倒なようにもみえるが，これがないことには，事務効率がさっぱり上がらないのである。

→辞表

根回し

本来的には，植木職人が大きな木を移植するまえに，準備として根っこの回りを掘って，太い根を切り，小さい根を出させることである。ここから転じて，正式決定に先立って，関係者に支持を求めたり，内々に同意をとりつけるため，地ならししておくことをいう。

日本の社会は，集団の決定やコンセンサスで動く。だから「根回し」は，コンセンサス作りに欠かせぬ手順である。正面きった対決を回避することにもなる。

open confrontation. In the United States, there is a similar process known as pre-selling, but a decision may be taken regardless of whether or not everyone concerned is in agreement.

In Japan, a proposal will be revised in the process of **nemawashi** until it is moulded into a form which is acceptable to all. So much time is spent in **nemawashi** that foreign businessmen often become exasperated waiting for a Japanese company to make a decision.

→ **Ringi**

Newaza-shi

A person who is skilled in behind-the-scenes negotiations is known as a **newaza-shi.** It derives from the **jūdō** term **newaza** which is an offensive technique used by a contestant lying on the mat.

As can be imagined, with his bagful of plays, the **newaza-shi** often engineers an unexpected reversal which completely changes the complexion of things. At other times, with his clandestine maneuverings, he makes possible things which seemed impossible for those operating in the limelight. If a man is known as a **newaza-shi**, he can be relied upon to spring a surprise.

Nippachi

In a strict sense, **nippachi** is not a word because it is composed of two figures — 2 and 8. The figures stand for the 2nd month and the 8th

アメリカでも，これに似たやり方に pre-selling（事前の売込み）というのがある。しかし，アメリカでは，全員が納得するしないにかかわりなく，決定を下してかまわない。

日本では，ある案件について，根回ししてゆくうちに，修正を加えて，全員に受け入れられるような方式のものにする。だから根回しには時間がかかる。外国のビジネスマンは，日本の会社でなかなか決定が出ないため，しびれを切らしてしまうことがよくある。

→稟議

寝わざ師

舞台裏の駆け引きにたけた人を「寝わざ師」という。柔道の寝技からきたことば。試合で，畳に寝たような状態で相手を攻める技（わざ）である。

これから分かるように，寝わざ師は，豊富な術策を用いて，しばしば，物事の情況を完全に変えてしまうような，思いがけない逆転をもたらす。また，秘密の策動をして，表面でそれにたずさわっている人には不可能と思われることを可能にする。

「あの人は寝わざ師だ」という評判があるなら，その人は，意表をつくようなことをするだろうと期待できる。

二八（にっぱち）

厳密にいうと，にっぱちは，ちゃんとしたことばではない。ふたつの数字，2と8の組み合わせである。この数字は，1年の2番目の月と8番目の月，つまり， February

month of the year, or February and August.

Meteorologically, these are the coldest and the hottest months of the year in Japan. But the word has nothing to do with the weather. It is a business term, and refers to the fact that February and August are traditionally the months when business is slack in Japan.

"How's business?" you ask, and if it happens to be either February or August, the answer more often than not is "Well, you know, it's **nippachi**." It's so commonly accepted that **nippachi** is bad for business that it is quite often used as an acceptable excuse by people who want to put off a transaction or to delay paying their bills.

→ **Kaki-ire-doki**

Noren

In the old days, **noren**, a kind of cloth curtain (cotton or sometimes rope woven with hemp), was hung under the eaves of a house to ward off the sun and to serve as a blind. In the Edo Period (17th—19th C.) merchants dyed their shop name on the **noren** and hung it under the eaves as a signboard.

From this, the word began to be used to mean a store's reputation and its business rights. Although it may appear that Japan does not have the custom of concluding contracts, merchants made a promise saying "I stake my **noren** on ......

と August からきている。

　気象上からいうと，日本では2月がもっとも寒く，8月がもっとも暑い。しかし，にっぱちと気象のことは関係ない。商売用語なのである。昔から2月と8月は商売がひまな月であることをいう。

　「景気はどうですか？」たまたま2月か8月だったら，判で押したように，こんな答えが返ってくる。「にっぱちですからねえ」にっぱちは景気が悪い，と相場が決まっている。だから，取引を先に延ばしたいとき，支払いを待ってもらいたいとき，よく口実に使われる。にっぱちじゃ，やむを得ない，というわけだ。

　→書き入れ時

のれん（暖簾）

　軒先に吊して日よけ，目かくしとする布（しゅろ，麻を編んだ縄ののれんもある）だが，江戸時代の商家で軒先に商店名（屋号）を染めて吊す店の看板であった。

　転じて店の信用や営業権などを意味するようになった。日本では契約の習慣が無かったようにみえるが，「のれん

...''. This was like entering into a contract by giving as security his entire personality and his entire reputation. Anyone who behaved in a way to ''sully his **noren**'' was treated like an incompetent person. The **noren** was truly the merchant's face. It is similar to regimental colors. Today, a company's credit and social reputation can be considered as its **noren**.

In the old days, it was the practice to ''divide the **noren**''(**noren-wake**) which meant giving a clerk with long service a **noren** with the same mark and same name as the master's store to open a separate shop. At times the master gave the clerk financial aid and even some of his own customers. This is somewhat similar to the relationship between the modern franchiser and franchisee.

Õbune ni noru

One doesn't have to be a sailor to know that navigating on rough seas is safer and more comfortable on a big ship (**õbune**) than on a small boat. Thus, the greenhorn businessman would feel as if he were riding (**noru**) on a big ship when he is assigned to a project which is under the charge of a veteran reputed for his ability.

にかけて……」の約束は，その商人の全人格・全信用を担保にしての契約ともいえるものであった。「のれんを汚す」行為は，現代では禁治産者扱いされるに等しい。正に，のれんは商人の顔であり，軍人にとっての軍旗であった。現在ではのれんに当たるものは，会社の信用，社会的評価などか。

なお，かつて「のれん分け」として古くからの番頭に同名・同印ののれんを与え，独立の分店を開かせることがあり，ばあいにより資金援助や得意先も分けることがあった。現代でのフランチャイザーとフランチャイジーに似ていよう。

大船に乗る

荒天の海をゆくには，小さな舟より大きな船（big ship）の方が安全だし，安心できることくらい，船乗りでなくても知っている。まだ新米のビジネスマンが，腕ききの評判高いベテラン先輩の指揮する部課に配属されると，大きな船に乗っているようなものである。

When somebody can rest at ease in the knowledge that things will go well because the business in which he is involved is in the hands of a capable person, or because he is one cog in a large, smoothly running machine, he feels that he is on an **ōbune**.

Thus the term can be used to mean "to just tag along and don't worry about anything".

Ocha wo nomu

Probably no other people **ocha wo nomu** so frequently during office hours as do the Japanese. Literally translated, it means "drink (**nomu**) tea (**ocha**)," but the expression is used also to cover coffee.

The first thing company workers do when they arrive at the office in the morning is to drink green tea. Tea is again served at mid-morning and mid-afternoon. As soon as a visitor to the office is seated, he is served green tea. Tea is served also at business meetings.

Very frequently, co-workers go out during office hours to a neighboring coffee shop to **ocha wo nomu**. The purpose usually is a tete-a-tete. So, when a person asks a fellow worker, "**Ocha wo nomi-masenka?**" ("How about a cup of tea?"), he is saying, "Let's just the two of us have a chat". And the chat usually is about personnel matters. Very often, drinking tea together

自分のやっている仕事には有能な人がついていてくれる
から，うまくいくに違いないと気楽に構えていられるとき，
あるいは，順調に動いている大きな機械の歯車のひとつだ，
と思っているとき，「大船に乗って」いる気がする。

　そこで，「ただ，ついていきさえすれば，なにも心配す
ることはない」といった意味につかう。

お茶を飲む

　日本人は，勤務時間中によくお茶を飲む。直訳すると，
drink（飲む）tea（お茶）であるが，コーヒーを飲んでも，
「お茶を飲む」といえる。

　勤め人が，朝オフィスにつく。まず第一にお茶を飲む。
あと，10時すぎと午後3時ごろにもお茶が出る。来客でお
茶，会議でもお茶だ。

　よく同僚を誘って，勤務時間中に会社を抜け出しては近
くの喫茶店へ行ってお茶を飲む。目的は大体おしゃべりを
することだ。そこで，同僚に「お茶を飲みませんか」（How
about a cup of tea？）と聞かれたら，ああ，あの人は，
ふたりだけでおしゃべりしたくて誘っているのだな，と察
する。このようなときのおしゃべりは，ふつう人事のうわ
さである。しばしば，お茶を飲むのは，情報交換の大切な

serves as an important way of exchanging information.

Business discussions with clients, too, are also frequently held over **ocha** in a coffee shop.

Odawara-hyõjõ

Odawara-hyõjõ is something which the contemporary world has come to expect of international conferences dealing with controversial political and economic problems. Way back in 1590, when the forces of warlord Toyotomi Hideyoshi attacked Odawara Castle, the stronghold of Hõjõ Ujinao, a war council was held by the besieged forces to discuss whether to resist to the end or to negotiate for a truce. The discussions went on and on without reaching a decision. Since that time, **Odawara-hyõjõ** has become a synonym for fruitless debate, inconclusive conferences and generally endless talk resulting in nothing.

Õgosho, Insei

Originally, **õgosho** meant the residence of a retired **shõgun** (feudal military governor) and **insei** the system under which a retired emperor continued to rule. Today, the former term is used mostly to mean the most prominent and influential figure, "the grand old man" in a certain sector of society — industry, letters, medicine, sports,

場となっている。

　お客と商売の話をするときも，喫茶店で「お茶を飲みながら」ということがよくある。

小田原評定

　「小田原評定」は，現代世界でもややこしい政治・経済問題を討議する国際会議によくみられる。語源は 1590 年に遡る。この年，豊臣秀吉の軍勢が，小田原城にたてこもった武将，北條氏直の軍勢を攻めたとき，北條方の城中で，戦うか和議を結ぶかの相談がなかなかまとまらなかった。評定は延々とつづき，一向に結論が出なかった。ここから，「小田原評定」とは，実りない議論，結論が出ずにだらだらした会議，なにも生まれないまま果てしなく続く話し合い，のことを指すようになった。

大御所，院政

　もともと，「大御所」とは隠居した公卿や将軍のいる所から，その人への尊称となった。「院政」とは，退位した天皇がなお政治を執ること。いまは，「大御所」というと，もっとも卓越した，勢力ある人物。組織やある種の業界——実業界，文学・医学・スポーツ界などで，その道の長老

etc. The **ōgosho** is universally recognized as truly a man of big stature. He may be retired or he may still be active.

Insei today refers to a situation in which a person continues to wield great power in an organization or field from which he has already retired. He is able to do this because his successor is weak and is dependent on him or because he built up an especially strong personal power base before he officially retired from his post.

Ohako

Ohako is an art or a skill in which one excels. In other words, it means one's forte or speciality. The reference is to something specific rather than general. For instance, one's **ohako** would not be the general "playing golf" but the specific "putting". Some golfer's **ohako** may be to hit a bunker every time. At a party, participants are often called upon to perform their **ohako**, which may be a song, a sleight of hand or some other trick.

The Chinese characters for **ohako** can also be read **jūhachiban**, meaning No. 18. The original expression, which is still used today, is **Kabuki jū-hachiban**, meaning the 18 best plays in the repertoire of the Ichikawa family of Kabuki actors. How did the characters for 18 come to be read **Ohako**, which literally means "honorable box"? One theory is that the Ichikawa family carefully

をさす。大御所は，衆目の一致するところ，文句なしの人物で，現役か否かはとくに関係ない。

　院政は，もう隠退したのに，組織なり，その道でなお大きな勢力を振るっていること。後任者が弱体で，その人を頼りにしているとか，在任中に権力基盤をがっちり築き上げてしまったため，引退後もなお実力を残しているようなばあいである。

おはこ（十八番）

　「おはこ」は，秀でた芸なり技能をいう。いいかえれば，得手とか特殊技能である。全体的なことでなく，そのなかの特殊なことを指す。たとえば，ある人のおはこというとき，「ゴルフをやる」という全体のことではなく，なかでも「パット」がうまい，といった特定の技を指す。バンカーへかならず球を打ち込むのがおはこのゴルファーもいる。宴席でも，参加者におはこをやって，とせがむ。歌あり，手品あり，お座敷芸ありだ。

　「おはこ」を漢字で書くと「十八番」（No. 18）である。もとは「歌舞伎十八番」で，いまもある演題である。もともとは，歌舞伎俳優の市川家に伝わるお家芸の18の狂言を指した。十八番と書いて，どうしておはこ（honorable box）と読むのだろう。一説には，市川家では，この十八の

kept the manuals on how to act the 18 plays in a box (**hako**).

→ **Kakushi-gei**

Osumitsuki

This is a term which originated in Japan's feudal days. It referred to a formal paper signed by the **shōgun** or feudal lord, certifying that the bearer had been granted a certain authority or privilege. It was a sort of credential that was absolute, coming as it did from the highest power in the land.

Today, the term is used in a popular and informal sense to indicate that a person or a thing has received a stamp of approval, guarantee or support from some authoritative party.

A subordinate asks his manager about a promotion rumor. The superior says, "The rumor is correct. In the next personnel reassignment, I shall promote you to sub-manager." The subordinate can then say that he has received the **osumitsuki** of his superior. In such cases, the manager would not say he gives **osumitsuki**; it is the subordinate who says he receives it.

Ringi

Ringi is the system of circulating an intra-office memorandum (**ringi-sho**) to obtain the approval of all concerned for a proposed course of action

出し物の演じ方を秘伝として大切に箱（box）にしまって
おいたからだという。

　→かくし芸

おすみつき

　封建時代に生まれたことばである。将軍とか領主が署名
した正式の文書で、これを所持するものには、ある権限な
り特権が与えてあるという証明書である。一種の信任状で、
領国の最高権力者が発行したので、絶対のものであった。

　今日では、もっと広く、くだけた意味につかう。ある人
なり事柄が、権威ある当事者の承認、保証ないし支持を受
けていることを指す。

　部下が部長に昇進のうわさについて質問する。部長は
「そのうわさは本当だよ。次の人事異動で私は君を次長に
推してやるよ」といったとする。すると、部下は、偉い人
の「おすみつき」をもらったことになる。このようなばあ
い、部長は、おすみつきをやったとはいわず、ただ部下の
方がおすみつきをもらったという。

稟議（りんぎ）

　「稟議」とは、小はワードプロセッサーの購入から、大
は会社の合併に至るまで、予定案件について、関係者全員
の承諾をとりつけるため、部内に文書（稟議書）を回付す

which could range from, say, the purchase of a word processor to a merger. Corporate decisions and actions seldom take place without **ringi**.

Depending on the nature of the proposal, the **ringi-sho** may circulate vertically from the bottom up or horizontally among managers and directors of related sections and divisions before coming up to the managing director or the president, depending on the importance of the subject matter. It goes without saying that **nemawashi** is necessary before the **ringi-sho** is circulated. Each person puts a seal (**hanko**) of approval on it, which is the Japanese equivalent of the signature in the Western world.

The advantage of this system is that everyone becomes involved so that once a decision has been made, company-wide cooperation in its implementation is assured. Also, if anything goes wrong, responsibility is conveniently diffused so that nobody gets blamed.

→ **Hanko, Nemawashi**

Rõnin

Rõnin were the **samurai** of feudal days who, for one reason or another, were not in the service of a lord. Thus the word is usually translated as "masterless **samurai**". Today, a century after the **samurai** disappeared, there are still many **rõnin** in Japanese society.

る仕組みをいう。会社の意思決定なり措置が，なんらかの稟議抜きで行なわれることはまずない。

　提案の内容によって，稟議には，下から上にあがってゆくタテ型と，関係部課長の間に回されるヨコ型があり，最後には，事と次第によって専務なり社長のところへゆく。稟議書が回される前に根回しを十分にしておくことが大切である。関係者は承認したしるしに，それぞれ印鑑を押す。印鑑は欧米の署名と同じである。

　稟議制のいいところは，みんなが関与しているので，いったん決定が下されると，その実行に会社全体が協力する。うまくいかなかった場合でも，みんなの責任になるので，特定の人が傷つくことはない。

　→はんこ，根回し

浪人

　「浪人」は，封建時代になんらかの理由で仕官していないサムライをいう。訳せば masterless samurai（主君なきサムライ）というところか。サムライがいなくなった現代でも，日本にはまだ浪人がたくさんいる。

One type of modern-day **rõnin** is the high school graduate who fails to pass a university entrance examination and studies privately before trying his luck again the following year. There are tens of thousands of such youngsters, some of whom have been **rõnin** for two or three years.

Another type of **rõnin** is the person who is unemployed, not because no company would hire him, but because he is particular about the kind of work he wants to do. Such a person is voluntarily unemployed. Politicians who have failed in an election and who are preparing to run in the next one are also called **rõnin**.

Sãbisu

Although **sãbisu** is adopted from the English word "service", the Japanese have given it the meaning of "free", or "without charge" and "discount".

When the customer in a shop uses it as a verb saying, "**Sãbisu shite**", he means "Give me a discount." The clerk replies, "I can't make it any cheaper, but I'll **sãbisu** this," and offers a novelty as a gift or gives an extra quantity of the thing being purchased. When slightly damaged fresh foodstuffs are sold at a big discount, it is labelled in red as "**sãbisu** item".

Of course, when one says of a restaurant or a bar "the **sãbisu** is good/bad", the meaning is ex-

高校は出たけれど大学入試に失敗，来年に捲土重来を期して，ひとり勉強している学生も浪人である。こうした若者は何万といて，なかには2年，3年と浪人をつづけるものもいる。

もうひとつの浪人は，意に染まぬ仕事はしたくない，などの理由でみずから好んで"失業中"のばあいである。選挙に落ちて，次期出馬に備えている政治家もやはり浪人である。

サービス

もともとは英語の service から転じたものであるが，本来の言葉の意味のひとつ「無償の行為」から転じて日本語となったサービスは，「無料」ないし「値引き」を意味している。

小売店で買物のとき，客が「サービスして」とは「値引きして」の意味である。店は「値段はもう下げられませんが，これをサービスしておきましょう」と，小さな景品や商品の数量をわずかながら増して引き渡すなどしてサービスする。少々傷んだ生鮮食品を大幅に値引きして売るときなど「サービス品」と朱書したりする。

もちろんレストランやバーなどの「サービスが良い／悪

actly the same as the original English "service". Sometimes one sees a sign outside a restaurant saying, "Today is **Sābisu** Day", but this does not mean that the service will be good on that particular day. It means that a cup of coffee will be presented free of charge if you order such and such a dish or that a small discount will be given on such and such a dish.

—San

The Japanese don't have to worry whether they should address a woman as Mrs. or Miss. The suffix —**san**, is neuter gender and can be used for everybody. It can come after the family name, as in "Tanaka-**san**" or "Smith-**san**" or after the first name, as in "Hanako-**san**" or "Mary-**san**", although Japanese men do not call each other by the first name. Sometimes, it can be inconvenient because upon meeting Tanaka-**san**, you suddenly discover it's a she and not a he as you thought all along.

The suffix —**san** is also used with company names: "Mitsubishi-**san**". A superior usually does not call his subordinate —**san**. Nor do close friends address each other as —**san**. The suffix they use is —**kun**. Women friends, however, do not call each other —**kun**.

In a business organization, persons with titles are usually addressed only by their title, such as

い」というばあいは，英語本来の意味とまったく同じであるが，ときおりレストランの入口などに「本日サービスデー」などの札が下がっているばあいは，別にその日のサービスが良くなるわけではない。〜を注文したらコーヒーを無料にしますとか，〜料理は〜円値引きしますの意味なのである。

——さん

　日本人が女性に呼びかけるとき，Mrs. でいいのか，Miss なのか，気を遣う必要はない。接尾語の「さん」は中性なので，だれにでも使えるからだ。姓のあとにつけて田中さんとかスミスさん，名のあとにつけて花子さん，メアリーさんとなる。ただし，日本の男性がお互いに名（first name）で呼び合うことは少ない。「——さん」は不便なこともある。田中さんと初めて顔を合わせて「あっ，女性だったのか，男とばかり思っていたのに」なんてこともある。

　接尾語の「さん」は会社名にもつける。「三菱さん」といった具合だ。上司はふつう部下を「さん」付けにしない。親しい友達同士も，だれだれさんとはいわない。このばあいの接尾辞は「君」である。ただ女性にはやはり「——さん」である。

　会社組織では，役職にある人には，その職名だけで呼ぶ

buchõ (manager) or **shachõ** (president). It is not only in the office that this form of address is used. At year-end parties and on the golf course, too, people are addressed by their title. This may sound to people of the West like failing to draw a line between private and public life, but in Japan it is the accepted etiquette. This is because in the old days it was considered impolite to call a person by name.

→ **Bureikõ**

Seifuku

Tellers, typists, secretaries and all other female employees of banks work in company-provided uniforms — **seifuku**. So do girls with securities and insurance companies, department stores and super-markets. Almost all girls working in large Japanese companies wear uniforms either in offices or factories.

Of the top 2,000 Japanese companies, there are very few which do not provide uniforms for girls. But there are very few companies which provide uniforms for white collar male employees; they wear company badges on their suit lapels.

In the belief that the company uniform plays an important role in corporate image-making, more and more companies are using top designers including such international big names as Hanae

のがふつうだ。部長（manager）とか社長（President）といった風に，肩書きで相手を呼ぶのは会社内だけではない。忘年会などのパーティやゴルフ場などでも，すべて肩書きで呼ぶ。外国人には公私混同と思えるかもしれないが，会社以外でも肩書きで呼ぶことがむしろ礼儀にかなったこととされている。これは，昔，人を名前で呼ぶことは失礼とされていた名残である。

→無礼講

制服

　銀行では，窓口係，タイピスト，秘書など女子行員は，お仕着せのユニホーム「制服」を着る。証券会社や保険会社，デパート，スーパーでも同じだ。大会社に勤める女性も，ほとんど全員が，オフィスでも工場でも，お揃いのユニホームである。

　トップの企業2000社のうち，女性に制服を支給していないところは，ほんの僅かしかない。逆に男子の事務職に制服を着せている会社もめったにない。代わりに男子は，上衣の襟の折返しに会社のバッジを付けている所が多い。

　会社の制服は，その企業イメージにつながるところ大とあって，森英恵などの国際的に有名なデザイナーに頼む会

Mori to design their uniforms.　This pleases the
girls.

Sekigahara, Ten·nōzan

The battles of **Sekigahara** (1600) and **Ten·
nōzan** (1582) were, like the Battle of Waterloo,
decisive battles which changed the course of history.

Whereas Waterloo is used to mean a crushing
defeat, the emphasis of the Japanese names is on
a crucial contest or critical dividing point in the
course of events.　It was said that a person who
emerges victorious in **Sekigahara** or **Ten·nōzan**
becomes the ruler of **tenka** or all Japan.

The Japanese, who have a penchant for drama-
tizing things, are very fond of using these terms in
describing any kind of confrontation.　The final
decisive negotiations between management and
labor union on a pay increase is referred to as a
Ten·nōzan.　A struggle between two companies
for domination of a market is termed a **Sekigahara**.

Sekiji

Sekiji means the seating order at a formal
function.　This is something which also exists
in the Western society.　In addition, **sekiji** refers
to the order of rank in an organization such as a
company.　The person whose **sekiji** in the compa-

社がふえてきて，ギャルたちにも喜ばれている。

関が原，天王山

「関が原」（1600年）と「天王山」（1582年）の戦いは，ワーテルローと同じく，日本史の針路を変えるほどの決定的な戦いであった。

「ワーテルロー」は，潰滅的な敗北を指すときにつかうが，関が原と天王山は，関が原または天王山を制するものは天下を制すといわれるように，天下の命運を左右する戦いとか，事の成りゆきの重大なわかれ目をいう。

日本人は，物事を劇的なことになぞらえるのが好きで，なにか対決の様相をあらわすのに，こんな表現をよくつかう。労使の賃上げ交渉で決定的な最終段階を迎えるときが「天王山」であり，ふたつの会社が市場制覇を目指してしのぎあうのは「関が原」である。

席次

公式の席における坐る場所の順である。この意味において，欧米の公式宴会の席順とあまり違わない。席次のもうひとつの意味は，この宴会の席次に似た社内など組織内の序列のことを指す。組織内の席次の上の人は，宴会の席で

ny is higher sits closer to the head of the table at parties also.

In Japanese society, where the seniority system is the rule, generally the person who is older has a higher **sekiji**. If two persons have the same rank in the company, the person who rose to that rank earlier in point of time usually has a higher **sekiji**.

→ **Bureikō, Dõki**

Senpai and Kõhai

In the Japanese business world, one of the gambits used to influence a person is to approach him through his **senpai**. **Senpai** is a person who has preceded another in graduating from school, in joining a company or government service, in assuming a post, in acquiring an experience, etc. **Kõhai** is someone who follows in the footsteps of the **senpai**.

In Japan's seniority-conscious and paternalistic society, the **senpai-kõhai** relationship is of great importance. The **senpai** looks after the interests of the **kõhai** and the latter seeks help and advice from the former and respects his wishes.

A generation or so ago, the **senpai-kõhai** relationship was viable even if the two sides had never met previously. Nowadays, there is a perceptible dilution of the relationship in the cases where the two are not already acquainted with each other personally.

→ **Dõki, Jin·myaku**

も上に坐るわけだ。

年功序列の日本社会では，年齢が上なら一般に席次が上であり，役職が同じなら先任者が上席となることが多い。

→無礼講，同期

先輩 と 後輩

仕事の世界で，ある人に働きかけようとする場合に，まず，その人の「先輩」を通じてアプローチをするという手がつかわれる。「先輩」とは，学校の卒業年次とか，入社，入省，あるいは役職就任や経験の取得などで，相手よりも早い人をいう。「後輩」は先輩の歩んだ道をたどっている人である。

日本のように，年功序列の意識がつよく，家族主義的な社会では，先輩・後輩の関係はきわめて大切である。先輩は後輩の面倒をみる。

後輩は先輩の助けや忠言を仰ぎ，その意思を尊重する。30年ほど以前は，面識がなくても先輩・後輩の関係は生きていた。いまでは，先輩・後輩といっても，よく知らない間柄だと，その関係はかなり薄くなってしまった。

→同期，人脈

Shain-ryõ, Tanshin-ryõ

Large Japanese companies maintain dormitories called **shain-ryõ** for their employees. Multistoried dormitories for bachelor employees whose family homes are outside the city are known as **tanshin-ryõ**.

Companies which have many branches or facilities in various cities throughout the country maintain dormitories in each location to house employees transferred from another city.

The use of dormitories is voluntary and each company has its own regulations on the qualifications for occupancy. The communal dormitory life helps to generate affinity among the employees. The dormitory fee, usually a nominal sum, is deducted from the monthly pay.

Some companies provide independent housing for families which are called **sha-taku**.

→ — Chon, Tanshin-funin

Shain-ryokõ

Shain-ryokõ is one of the methods used in Japanese companies to strengthen group consciousness. It is the company excursion in which all executives and employees are expected to participate. In a large company, the excursion is held in divisional or even smaller groups so that all

社員寮，単身寮

日本の大会社は，従業員用に「社員寮」という寄宿舎を設備している。家族を遠くに残してひとりで赴任してきている従業員用の宿舎が「単身寮」である。

全国あちこちの都市に，大きな支店なり，施設のあるところでは，寮があって，他の地域から転勤してきた従業員の宿舎にあてている。

寮に入る，入らないは，自由であるが，ひとつ屋根の下に寝起きすれば，連帯意識が生まれる。寮費は，あまり高くはなく，月給から天引きされる。

企業によっては，家族用の一戸建て住宅を提供するところもある。これを「社宅」という。

→ ──チョン，単身赴任

社員旅行

社員旅行は，日本の企業内でグループ意識の高揚をはかるのにつかわれる方法のひとつである。"お偉方"も"ヒラ"も，全員参加する会社の旅行である。大会社では，部課単位，ないしそれ以下のグループで旅行し，皆が同じ旅館に

members can be accommodated at the same resort inn.

The main event is a big banquet where drinks flow freely and break down reserves. The informal atmosphere gives junior employees and secretaries a chance to talk and kid with their bosses. The party is enlivened by singing, impromptu skits and the like, with each person contributing some kind of performance. At night some of the participants, sometimes even a dozen or more, sleep side by side in the same room on the **tatami** (straw matting). On the following day, they usually go sightseeing.

→ **Bureikõ, Kakushi-gei**

Shain-shokudõ

Most large Japanese companies have within their premises a subsidized cafeteria where employees can eat lunch at prices considerably lower than in outside restaurants. Some **shain-shoku-dõ** offer a wide variety of dishes — Japanese, Chinese and Western. The modest ones offer only snack type food.

In addition to being cheap, the **shain-shokudõ** is convenient for those who are pressed for time

泊まれるようにする。

　ハイライトは大宴会だ。杯がどんどん回され，無礼講となる。くだけた雰囲気なので，"下っ端"の社員も秘書嬢も，ボスに話しかけたり，冗談もいえる。宴会は歌あり寸劇ありで，一段と盛りあがる。みんなが，なにがしかの芸を披露して興を添える。夜になると，何人かずつ，ときには十数人も相部屋になり，畳（straw matting）に床を並べて寝る。翌日は観光見物としゃれるのが相場だ。

　→無礼講，かくし芸

社員食堂

　大会社になると，社内にカフェテリアがある。会社が補助しているので，外のレストランよりも安く昼食がとれる。「社員食堂」には，メニューが豊富なところもある。和食あり，中華あり，洋食あり，といった具合だ。スナック式のものや一種類しか出さない簡単なところもある。

　社員食堂は，安いうえに，時間に追われている人，手っ

and must take a quick lunch. Not only the rank-and-file but also the managers and executives use the same company cafeteria. Usually, a catering company operates the cafeteria under the company's supervision.

Shaka

The story is told of how an early morning Western visitor to a world-famous Japanese corporation was astounded at the sight of assembled employees singing the **shaka** (company anthem) before starting the day's work. Not many companies go through this ritual, but quite a few companies have their own songs.

They are sung in chorus on such occasions as the first day of the year, the company anniversary and the opening of a new branch office. The **shaka** enhances the sense of belonging in much the same way as the uniforms of blue-collar and female workers and company badges worn by white-collar workers in their suit lapels.

Many companies also have corporate flags. Some Japanese companies have experimented with modern American corporate identity programs but they have found that the traditional methods are more effective for Japanese workers.

→ **Chõrei**

取り早く昼食をすまさねばならぬ人には便利である。一般社員ばかりではない。管理職も重役も，やはり社員食堂で同じ食事を共にする。社員食堂は会社の監督のもとに，専門の業者に委託することが多い。

社歌

　外国から訪ねてきた人が，朝早く，世界中に名の通った日本の会社に行ったときのこと，仕事を始めるまえに従業員が朝礼で「社歌」（ company anthem ）を合唱しているのをみて，びっくりした，という話をよく聞く。この儀式をやっている会社は，それほど多くないが，社歌のあるところは随分とたくさんある。

　年の始めとか，会社の創立記念日とか，新支店の開業式とかに社歌を合唱する。社歌も，工場従業員や女子職員の制服，男子社員の背広のバッジと同じように，会社との一体感を高揚するものである。

　「社旗」のある会社も多い。日本の会社でも，アメリカ流の帰属意識高揚法を実施しているところがあるが，やはり日本の勤労者には昔からのやり方が効果があるようだ。

　→朝礼

Shayõ-zoku

When this word is directly translated, it doesn't make sense because it comes out as "company business tribe". It refers to corporate employees who are privileged to live it up at the company's expense. The impression the word conveys is "expense-account plutocrats".

These are people holding positions which require them to do a lot of business entertaining and therefore have fat expense accounts. They are the best customers of plush restaurants, night clubs and bars. In fact, the business of many such establishments is solely dependent on the **shayõ-zoku**.

These people are usually envied but they can be an unhappy tribe when they are reassigned and return to paying out of their own wallets like other salaried employees.

→ **Kõsai-hi**

社用族

　直訳すると "company business tribe"。これでは，ちんぷんかんぷんだ。つまり，会社の経費で飲み食いできる特権社員のことである。語感からすると「交際費をたくさん使える人」といったところか。

　社用接待をあれこれやらねばならず，それだけに交際費伝票をいくらでも切れる地位にある人を指す。豪華なレストランやナイトクラブ，バーでは，下へもおかぬお得意様だ。事実，こうした店は「社用族」だけで商売が成り立っている。

　社用族を羨ましいとばかりはいえない。その部署が変わって，他のサラリーマンと同様，身銭を切らねばならぬ身分に戻ったとき，栄耀栄華一朝の夢をはかなむ仕儀となる。

　→交際費

Shaze, Shakun

Most Japanese companies have either a **shaze** or a **shakun** or both. **Sha** means company. **Ze** means what is right or justification. **Kun** means precept. **Shaze** means, therefore, a statement of corporate principles and ideals, and loosely corresponds to the motto of a Western corporation. **Shakun** is a statement of basic precepts or exhortations directed at company employees.

Shaze is usually tersely expressed in lofty, high-sounding, formalized language. **Shakun** sometimes takes the same form but is more often expressed in ordinary language.

The original is usually written in brush calligraphy, framed and hung up in the president's office or the board conference room. At some companies, it is customary for the employees to recite in unison the **shaze** or **shakun** every morning before starting work.

→ **Chõrei**

Shin·nyũ-shain

April is the month in which companies welcome into their fold the new crop of high school and university graduates. Although graduation is in spring, the recruits, known as **shin·nyu-shain** are almost all chosen by the end of the preceding year in the process known as **aota-gai**.

社是，社訓

　日本の会社は，たいてい社是とか社訓，またはその両方をもっている。「社」は company。「是」は what is right とか justification（正しいこと）。「訓」は precept（戒律）。ここから「社是」とは会社の原則や理想を宣言したもの。欧米の企業の「モットー」と思えばよい。「社訓」は従業員にたいする基本的な教えとか勧めを述べたもの。

　「社是」は簡潔高尚で仰々しく，いかめしいことばづかいであることが多い。だが「社訓」は，これに似ているが，もっと分かりやすいことばになっているばあいが多い。

　そもそもは墨筆で書かれ，額に入れて社長室や会議室に掲げられていた。会社によっては，毎朝の仕事始めに従業員が唱和するしきたりのところがある。

　→朝礼

新入社員

　4月は，どの会社もほやほやの高卒や大卒を社員に迎える月である。卒業は春だが，「新入社員」は，青田買いで前の年の終わりまでにほとんど全員が採用内定ずみになっている。

Every company holds a formal ceremony to welcome the recruits, with the president giving a speech to tell them what is expected of them and what they can expect from the company during their lifetime employment.

The recruits are then given a course of basic training during which the company spirit is hammered into them and they learn the general outline of the company's business. This training lasts anywhere from a week to a couple of months, depending on the company. In some cases, they enter a company retreat where they eat and sleep together to cement **dōki** ties. After the training period, they are assigned to various sections for on-the-job training to learn specific business skills.

→ **Aota-gai, Dōki**

Shita, Kuchi

For some reason, many of the Japanese expressions associated with man's tongue (**shita**) and mouth (**kuchi**) do not have a complimentary tone. For instance, there is the **nimai-jita** (double-tongued) person whose words cannot be trusted because he is a double-dealer or a liar.

Kuchi-guruma ni noseru (loosely: take a person on a ride on one's mouth wheel) is to take a person in with sweet talk.

Kōzetsu no to, where **kō** is the phonetic reading of the character for mouth and **zetsu** that for

どの会社も新入社員歓迎式を行ない，社長が訓示する。これからの会社生活で，会社は社員になにを期待するか，会社から何が期待できるか，を説く。

新入社員は，このあと研修を受ける。この期間に会社の精神を叩き込まれ，会社の事業のあらましを頭に入れる。この研修は，会社によって1週間ないし数カ月もつづく。ときには会社の休養施設に "缶詰" にし，寝食をともにしながら同期の連帯感を固める。研修期間が終わると，各課に配属されて実地訓練を受け，仕事を身につける。

→青田買い，同期

舌，口

どういうわけか，「舌」(tongue) と「口」(mouth) に関係ある日本語の表現には，あまり褒めたことばでないものが多い。たとえば，あの人は「二枚舌」(double‐tongue) をつかうという。裏表があったり，嘘をつくので，いうことに信用がおけないことを指す。

「口車に乗せる」(しいて訳せば take a person on a ride on one's mouth wheel) とは，甘言で釣ること (to take a person in with sweet talk) である。

「口舌の徒」(kō は mouth, zetsu は tongue の音読み)

tongue, is a person who talks so much that he causes controversy.

Shitasaki-sanzun (tip of the tongue three inches) describes a person with a smooth tongue who usually uses it to explain away his mistake or failure glibly.

A complimentary expression using the word mouth is **kuchi hattchō te hattchō** (skilful with the mouth, skilful with the hand). This refers to a person who is voluble and eloquent as well as efficient in doing things.

If a person does something in an exceptional way, he makes people **shita wo maku** (roll up the tongue) or astonishes them.

A modern expression which is a good example of the ingenious way in which Japanese adapt and assimilate foreign words is **kuchi-komi**. **Komi** is a corruption of the English word communication. Thus, this combination of Japanese and corrupted English translates as "mouth communication" or "by word of mouth".

Shitsurei shimasu

Shitsurei shimasu is a very convenient expression for a foreign resident in Japan to learn. It is a polite expression which is used in those situations and occasions when in English a person would say, "excuse me, but ...", "by your leave ...", "with your permission ...", "with all due

といえば，口先がうまく，禍を起こす人。

「舌先三寸」（tip of the tongue three inches）とは，ことばたくみにしゃべること，自分の間違いや失敗をいいくるめて，ごまかしてしまうこと。

口をつかった婉曲な表現には「口八丁，手八丁」（skilful with the mouth, skilful with the hand）がある。弁舌さわやかで，しかも，やることもきちんとしている人のこと。

なにかすぐれたことをした人には「舌を巻く」（roll up the tongue）。つまり感嘆する（astonish）。

外国語を採り入れて同化してしまうのは，日本人のお家芸だ。新感覚の表現には，これが多い。その一例に「口コミ」がある。「コミ」は英語の communication の変造。これに日本語の「口」を組み合わせて mouth communication つまり by word of mouth である。

失礼します

「失礼します」は，日本にいる外国人が知っていて便利なことばである。礼を失しないいい方である。英語でいう次のような状況やばあいにつかう。"excuse me, but……"，"by your leave……"，"with your permission……"，

respect to you ...", "allow me to take the liberty", "sorry to interrupt you". Thus, a visitor can use it both on entering and leaving somebody else's office.

It is also used in an entirely different context to mean simply "good-bye" or "well, I must be going now". In this second meaning, **shitsurei shimasu** is used more often than **sayonara** in everyday situations by the person who is taking leave. However, when you are saying good-bye at the airport upon your departure, **sayonara** is the word.

→ **Kekkō desu, Dōmo**

Shukkō-shain

In Japan, the mobility of white-collar workers is very low. When people join a company, they intend normally to stay with that company until the compulsory retirement age. But sometimes the management temporarily assigns an employee to work in another company. Such an employee is called a **shukkō-shain**.

Usually he works on a loan basis, with the understanding that he will be given the chance of returning to his original company. However, some persons choose to stay with the new company for the rest of their lives.

Senior executives are loaned to subsidiaries for support purposes. Banks loan executives as fi-

"with all due respect to you……", "allow me to take the liberty", "sorry to interrupt you……"

　部屋などに入るときも「失礼します」という。逆に、「さようなら」（goodbye）とか「もう、おいとましなくちゃ」（well, I must be going now）といった意味でも使われる。このばあいに「失礼します」は、「さようなら」よりもひんぱんにつかわれる。外国のビジネスマンは、日本人を訪ねて辞去するときとか、パーティから帰るとき、「失礼します」といえばよい。しかし、空港で見送りにきてくれた人達に goodbye をいうなら「失礼します」でなく「さようなら」である。

　　→結構です、どうも

出向社員

　日本では、事務系統の人が会社を変わることはめったにない。ある会社に入ると、ふつうは定年までそこで働くつもりでいる。しかし、会社側がある従業員を一時ほかの会社勤務に回すことがある。回された従業員を「出向社員」という。

　ふつうはもとの会社に戻すという約束で貸し出すわけだが、そのまま最後まで新しい会社に居残る人もいる。

　専任重役でも、子会社強化のために出向する。銀行は、融資先の会社に、経理担当として重役を出向させる。製造

nance officers to companies they finance. Manufacturers loan sales engineers to distributors. Central government agencies loan officials to local government agencies and industry associations.

One might say that the **shukkõ-shain** system is a sort of substitute for the executive recruiting which is normal in other countries.

→ **Ama-kudari**

Shūshin-koyõ

Much has been said about the advantages — both to the company and the employee — of the Japanese lifetime employment (**shūshin-koyõ**) system. Although the system offers security to the worker, it also makes it extremely difficult for a person to change his employment.

For the individual, it is vitally important to join a good company upon graduation from school. For management, it is vitally important to secure good quality people who will be useful for the next 35 years or so. This means that the competition to recruit and to gain admission to a company is very severe.

会社は，流通部門に，販売の専門家を出向させる。中央政府機関は，地方自治体や業界団体に，役人を出向させる。

出向社員制度は，一種の管理職スカウトみたいなものだが，他の国では珍しいことではない。

→天下り

終身雇用

日本の「終身雇用」制度（lifetime employment system）は，会社にとっても従業員にとっても，雇用の安定を保証してくれる。しかし，同時に，中途で会社を変えにくい。

その人にとって，学校卒業と同時に良い会社に入るのは，きわめて重要である。会社にとっても，この先35年くらい働いてもらうのだから，役に立つ有能な人材を確保するのはきわめて重要である。それだけに，入社試験を受け，採用になるのは，厳しい競争ということになる。

173

The era of low-growth economy has begun to expose one of the drawbacks of the lifetime employment system. Companies having to keep on their payroll old employees whose salaries are high but whose usefulness has declined are beginning to suffer. Thus the **kibō-taishoku** system has been introduced.

→ **Chūto-saiyō, Kibō-taishoku, Teinen**

Sode-no-shita

When a person gives money **sode-no-shita**, he is doing so "under-the-sleeve" — furtively, secretly, underhandedly. Thus, it is the Japanese counterpart of "under-the-table". To bribe a person is **sode-no-shita wo tsukau**. To accept a bribe is **sode-no-shita wo morau** or **ukeru**. To be corruptible or bribable is **sode-no-shita no kiku**.

Japanese government officials are said to be hard to bribe. Thus, when a case of bribery is exposed, even though it may be a small case involving an insignificant sum of money, it is usually given a big play by the mass media.

The accepted Japanese way of expressing appreciation for special favors received is to send gifts in the traditional gift-giving seasons of **ochū-gen** (mid-summer) and **oseibo** (year-end).

低成長時代とともに，終身雇用制の欠陥が目につきはじめてきた。会社としては，給料が高い割に有用度の落ちてきている高年齢者を抱えておかねばならないとあって，痛手を感じるようになった。そこで導入されるのが，希望退職制度である。

　→中途採用，希望退職，定年

袖の下

　「袖の下」とは，under‐the‐sleeves —— 内密に，こっそりと，隠れて金を渡すこと。英語の under‐the‐table を日本語に訳すと「袖の下」になる。賄賂を贈るのを「袖の下をつかう」という。収賄は「袖の下をもらう」または「受ける」。汚職したり，賄賂が通ずる人は「袖の下のきく」人である。

　日本の官吏は，賄賂がききにくく，清潔である。収賄が発覚すると，金品もわずかで，大したこともやっていないのに，マスコミで大々的に叩かれてしまう。

　特別の配慮を受けたことにお礼を表わす方法としては，昔からの「お中元」（mid‐summer）と「お歳暮」（year‐end）の贈答シーズンに贈物をすれば，それでよい。

Sõritsu-kinenbi

Japanese companies attach importance to the anniversary of their foundation (**sõritsu-kinenbi**). Big milestones, such as the 10th, 20th, 25th, 50th, etc. are usually celebrated with a big anniversary party.

The president makes a speech to thank suppliers, contractors, banks and employees for their help and support in making the company what it is. The company song and three shouts of **banzai** (Long Live the Company!) conclude the formal ceremony. Then employees and guests are served **sake**, the rice wine, and the festive red bean rice. Shareholders receive a bonus dividend.

In recent years it has become fashionable to publish the company history on big anniversaries. Not uncommon today is the substitution of the formal ceremony with an employee athletic meeting or a special paid leave.

→ **Shaka**

Soroban

Before the advent of the electronic calculator, the abacus (**soroban**) was in the attache case of the Japanese businessman as he travelled all over the world buying raw materials or selling

創立記念日

日本の会社は「創立記念日」(the anniversary of their foundation) を重視する。10周年，20周年，25周年といった大きな節目に，盛大な創立記念パーティを開いて祝う。

社長が挨拶する。会社を今日あらしめてくれた援助と支援にたいして納入業者，下請業者，銀行，従業員に感謝の意を表する。社歌の合唱と "ばんざい"（Long Live the Company！） 三唱で式をしめくくる。このあと，社員と来賓者一同に酒（rice wine）とお祝いの赤飯が振る舞われる。株主には臨時増配が出る。

近年は，大きな節目の記念日に，社史を出版するのが流行になっている。今日では，形式ばった式典に変わって，社員運動会とか特別有給休暇で祝うのも珍しくない。

→社歌

そろばん（算盤）

電卓が発明されるまで，日本のビジネスマンは，原料の買付けやら製品の売込みで世界中を飛び歩くとき，アタッシュケースに「そろばん」(abacus) を忍ばせていたもの

manufactured goods.   The abacus made the Japanese wizards at adding, subtracting, multiplying and dividing figures of multiple digits.

The assumption   that the electronic calculator and computer have made the abacus a museum piece is given the lie by the fact that in 1981 there were more than 10,000   private **soroban** schools run mostly by individuals, an increase of more than 3,000 in five years,   and that hundreds of thousands of youngsters take the annual examinations to obtain the official **soroban** accounting   certificate of the Japan Chamber of Commerce.

The operation of the abacus is regarded as good not only for developing mathematical ability but also for general mental training. The word **soroban** is used in a number of expressions to mean profitable, mercenary, commercially minded, etc.

Sumimasen

This is the Japanese equivalent of "I'm sorry" or "Excuse me". Although the original sense of the word is an expression of apology for having done something wrong, it has several other common uses.

It can be used to call the attention of a person when you don't know his name.   Addressing a waitress to place an order or addressing someone in the street to ask for directions is a typical use

である。そろばんのおかげで，日本人は幾ケタもの加減乗除の名人になった。

電卓やコンピュータができたので，そろばんも博物館行きとお思いだろう。ところが，あにはからんや，なのである。1981年にそろばん塾は1万軒以上もあり，5年間で3000カ所以上もふえた。日本商工会議所の公認そろばん検定試験を受けた人は数十万人にものぼった。

そろばんをはじくと，計数能力が発達するばかりでなく，精神修養にもいい，とされている。そろばんには，儲かるとか，計算高いとか，商売気が強い，といった意味もある。

すみません

"I am sorry." とか"Excuse me." にひとしい。元来「すみません」とは，なにかまずいことをしたときに陳謝の意を表わすことばである。しかし別の意味によくつかう。

名前も知らぬ人に呼びかけるとき，ウエイトレスに注文するとき，道で方角を尋ねるときが「すみません」の典型

of **sumimasen**. It can also be used as an informal "Thank you".

Sumimasen sometimes means "Please" when asking someone to do something. Suppose you visit someone at his office, you might say to the receptionist, **"Sumimasen** (Excuse me), I'd like to see Mr. Hara." **"Sumimasen** (Please) show me how to get to his office." **"Sumimasen** (Thank you)" and then to Mr. Hara, **"Sumimasen** (Sorry) I kept you waitiing."

→ **Dõmo, Chotto**

Sune-kajiri

One often hears people talking about a young man who is "gnawing at (his father's) shins" (**sune-kajiri**). It means that the young man, who is old enough to earn his own living, is still dependent financially on his father.

的なつかい方である。形式ばらずに「感謝します」をいうのにもつかう。

なにかをして欲しいときには，どうぞ（please）の意味で「すみません」である。ある人を会社に訪ねる。受付で「すみません（Excuse me），原さんにお会いしたいのですが」「すみません（please），その部屋にはどう行ったらいいのですか」「すみません」（Thank you）といって原さんのところへゆく。「すみません（Sorry），お待たせしてしまって」

　→どうも，ちょっと

スネかじり

よく「あいつは親父の"スネかじり"（gnawing at＜his father's＞ shins ）だ」などといういいかたを耳にする。その若者は，自分で一人前にかせげる年頃になっているのに，まだ経済的に親にたよっている，という意味である。

A couple of generations ago when Japanese wages were still very low, it was difficult for a young man just out of school to live on his starting pay. In those days **sune-kajiri** was quite common and not a stigma.

As Japan became economically affluent, starting wages rose and today young men just starting to work receive enough pay to cover their own living expenses. Thus the new breed of **sune-kajiri** sons are those who do not take up an occupation after graduating from school but pursue some special study or those who spend their wages for play and depend on their father for meals and a roof over their heads.

Suri-awase

If one should thoughtlessly place a new Japanese teacup or bowl on the table, it could result in a scratch on the surface of the table. This is because the rim on the underside of chinaware is not glazed. Therefore, whenever Japanese housewives buy new chinaware they rub the bottoms of two bowls together to smoothen their rims. This process is called **suri-awase**.

From this, the word is used to describe the process of adjusting different viewpoints among members of a group through mutual concessions in order to coordinate and unify the opinion of the group as a whole. Similarly, the adjustment

数世代も昔，まだ日本の賃金がとても低かったころ，学校出たての若者は初任給ではとても食べてゆけなかった。この時代には，「スネかじり」はごくあたりまえのことで，別に恥ではなかった。

　日本が経済的に豊かになるにつれて，初任給も上がり，社会に出たばかりでも，自立してゆけるだけの給料がもらえるようになった。そこで，新種の「スネかじり」息子が出てきた。学校を出ても定職につかず，なにか特別の勉強をやっている連中とか，もらった給料は遊びにつかって，食住は親におんぶ，という連中のことである。

すりあわせ

　湯呑み茶椀の糸底は，上薬がかけられていないものがあり，うっかり卓上に置くと，机の表面を傷つけてしまうことがある。だから，新しい陶器を買ってきたら，まず糸底同士を「すりあわせ」て，机などを傷つけないようにしなければならない。

　このことから，グループ内メンバー個々の意見の相違点を調整し，相互に譲歩しながらグループ全体の意見一致を図ることを「すりあわせ」と呼んでいる。またグループ相

of views between different groups is also sometimes called **suri-awase.** The former can also be called **nemawashi** and the latter may be described as "bargaining". At any rate, the prerequisite is that differences are not too great, as can be presumed from the fact that the term originally means rubbing the bottoms of the same kind of bowl.

The word is used also in political circles for adjusting views within the same party, but it is not applicable to the diplomatic world.

→ **Nemawashi**

Tana-oroshi

Here is a word which should be in the vocabulary of any foreign businessman selling goods in Japan. Literally meaning to take down (**oroshi**) from the shelf (**tana**), it is the Japanese term for stocktaking or inventory making. Book inventory is **chõbo-tana-oroshi**; inventory loss is **tana-oroshi-zon**.

The original meaning of taking down from the shelf and making an accounting has been twisted in social usage to mean "find faults, pick holes, run down, criticize, disparage". The favorite pastime of many men is to subject members of the fair sex to **tana-oroshi**.

互間の意見調整も「すりあわせ」ということもある。前者は根回しともいえるし，後者は交渉事ともいえようが，いずれにしろ，同じ茶椀の底をすりあわせるように，もともとあまり大きな相違点のないことが前提だろう。

政治用語としても使われるこのことばは，せいぜい党内意見調整程度で，外交用語としては無理なようである。

→根回し

棚おろし

日本に商品を売り込む外国ビジネスマンが是非知っておかねばならないことばがある。それは「棚おろし」である。文字どおりの意味は，棚（shelf）からおろす（take down）こと。stocktaking，inventory のこと。「帳簿棚おろし」が book inventory，「棚おろし損」は inventory loss である。

棚からおろして勘定する，という，もとの意味が，比喩的につかわれると，欠点を探す（find faults），あらを捜す（pick holes），けちをつける（run down），批判する（criticize），そしる（disparage），という風に変わる。男の暇つぶしで最大の話題は，女の子の棚おろしであろう。

Tanshin-funin

Tanshin-funin means "going to another city or country, unaccompanied by one's family, in order to take up a new post". **Tanshin-funin** is very common among middle-aged Japanese business-men with children of high school age. Under the Japanese educational system, it is extremely dis-advantageous for a boy or girl already in a high school to change schools. Thus, the father who is posted to a place away from home leaves his fami-ly behind and lives the life of a bachelor.

One might say that **tanshin-funin** is a descrip-tion of a "business bachelor." The term is not used of an unmarried person. Some corporations are understanding enough to give the "business bachelor" a special allowance to maintain a sep-arate household.

→ — **Chon, Shain-ryō**

Being the part of the body which is the most useful to man, **te** (hand) figures in a great number of expressions.

When you diversify and start a new line of busi-ness it is **atarashī shōbai ni** (new business) **te wo tsukeru.** To conduct that new business you take steps (**te wo utsu**) such as obtaining a bank loan

単身赴任

　「単身赴任」とは新しいポストにつくため，家族を同伴せずに，別の都市または別の国に赴任することである。単身赴任は，高校へゆく年頃の子供をもつ中年サラリーマンによくみられる。日本の教育制度では，すでに高校にあがっている子供が転校するのは，とても不利である。そこで，遠く離れた任地に赴任する父親は，家族をあとに残し，ひとりの生活を送る。

　「単身赴任者」は「ビジネス独身者」である。独身といっても，未婚の独身とは違う。会社によっては，家計が別別になるので，「ビジネス独身者」に特別手当支給の配慮をするところもある。

　→──チョン，社員寮

手

　体のもっとも重要な部分である手（hand）をつかった表現は実にたくさんある。ここでは，ほんの数例をあげるにとどめる。

　事業をひろげるとか，新規に始めるとき，新しい商売（new business）に「手をつける」。その商売の資金手当てをするため，銀行に「手を打っ」て融資を求める。必要な

or recruiting personnel. It means taking a move to ensure that a necessary thing will be done. **Te wo utsu** can also mean strike a deal or close a purchase or negotiate a sale. **Te wo hiku** is withdraw (for instance from a deal).

In drawing up a contract, you make sure that there is no **te-ochi** (slip, careless error, oversight). If something goes wrong with the contract, it will be your **te-ochi** (your fault, your blame).

In negotiations, you try to find out the other side's **te no uchi** (inside of the palm = intentions) before you show your hand (**te no uchi wo mise-ru**). If the other party is obstinate, unreasonable and uncompromising, he is **te ni amaru** (too much for the hand = intractable, unmanageable). So you throw up your hands in dismay (**o-te-age**) which can mean to give up or to be at a loss what to do. Experiencing so much difficulty or trouble (**te wo yaku**), you might want to **te wo kiru** (cut off the hand = stop dealing with, cut off connections) with that party.

In manufacturing your product for the Japanese market, it is best that you do not **te wo nuku** because the Japanese consumer is very particular. It means "cut corners" in its bad sense — economize on labor be careless or skip over a process.

Teate

The monthly salary of most Japanese corporate

ことを確実にやれるように措置する意味につかう。たとえば売買交渉の決着をつけるのも「手を打つ」である。その支払いを「手形」（bill）で受け取るといったいい方もある。「手を引く」は中止である。

　契約書を作るとき、「手落ち」（slip, careless error, oversight）がないかどうか確かめる。契約書に間違いがあれば、あなたの「手落ち」になる（your fault, your blame）。

　交渉では、自分の「手の内をみせる」(show your hand)まえに、相手の「手の内」(inside of the palm = intentions)を探ろうとする。相手が頑固（obstinate)で、分からず屋（unreasonable)で、妥協しない（uncompromising)と、「手に余る」(too much for the hand = intractable, unmanageable)。そこで、あきらめて「手をあげる」。すなわち、「お手上げ」（give up, at a loss what to do）となる。たいへんな困難や厄介事にぶつかって「手を焼く」(experiencing so much difficult or trouble)と、もう「手を切り」(cut the hand = stop dealing with, cut off connections)たくなる。

　日本市場向けの製品を作るとき決して「手を抜い」てはならない。日本のお客は目がこえているからだ。「手を抜く」とは、cut corner の悪い意味で、手間を省いたり（economize on labor)、きちんと気を配らなかったり、工程をとばすことをいう。

手当

　日本の会社員の月給は、たいてい2本立てである。いわ

employees consists of two parts — the so-called basic pay and the various allowances which are called **teate**. A list of the various types of **teate** would easily fill this page.

Some are based on the employee's private situation (allowance for dependents, housing allowance, etc.). Some are pegged to work (allowance for holding responsible or managerial posts, allowance for being an operator of a certain piece of equipment, overtime allowance, nightwork allowance, etc.).

This system makes it seem that the **teate** is something extra, over and above the regular pay. In practice, however, both employees and employers think of the **teate** as part of the monthly salary. Evidence of this is the general trend towards discontinuing the custom of breaking down the payment into basic pay and allowances and lumping them together as the monthly pay.

Teiki-saiyõ, Chūto-saiyõ

Japanese corporations make it a practice to recruit workers regularly once a year in spring, the time when high schools and universities graduate their students. This annual hiring is called **teiki-saiyõ**. The big corporations take in hundreds of graduates at the same time.

The hiring policy is not necessarily based on the need to fill a vacancy or to employ people to

ゆる本俸，それに「手当」と称するもろもろの賃金外給与
である。手当の項目を並べたら，このページがらくに一杯
になるほど，たくさんある。

　その人の個人的状況から割り出されるもの（扶養家族手
当，住宅手当など），仕事内容と結びついたもの（役職手
当，特殊機器操作手当，過勤手当，夜勤手当など）がある。

　この仕組みからわかるように，「手当」とは，決まった
給料とは別建てのものをいう。しかし，実際には従業員も
会社側も，手当を月給の一部とみなしている。その証拠に，
本俸と手当を別にわけて支給する習慣はなく，月給として，
込みで払うようになってきている。

定期採用，中途採用

　日本の会社は，年に一度，高校・大学卒業期の春に社員
採用するのがしきたりである。この採用を「定期採用」と
いう。大会社ともなると，何百人もの新卒をとる。

　採用はかならずしも空きを埋める必要があるからとか，
特定の仕事につける人達を雇うため，とはかぎらない。何

undertake specific tasks. How many people to hire is determined by each company's long-term strategic considerations.

If a company should find it necessary to hire people outside of the **teiki-saiyõ** process, the form adopted is called **chũto-saiyõ** (mid-way hiring). This may occur when a person with specialized knowhow is suddenly needed or when a company expands its operations and needs a large number of experienced people at once.

→ **Shin·nyũ-shain, hikinuki**

Teinen

Strictly speaking, the Japanese lifetime employment system does not guarantee lifelong employment. Employment terminates at the ages of 55, 57 or 60, depending on each company's employment regulations, whereas the average life expectancy of the Japanese male is up to the mid-70s. When the employee reaches the age for compulsory retirement (**teinen**), he automatically loses his job, regardless of his physical and mental condition or ability.

名採用するかは，それぞれの会社の長期の戦略的考慮から割り出される。

　会社が，定期採用の枠外で雇い入れる必要が生じたとき，「中途採用」する。特殊技能者を急に入用とするときとか，会社の事業拡大で経験ある人材を一度に大量に必要とするとき，中途採用が行なわれる。

　→新入社員，引き抜き

定年

　日本は終身雇用制だというが，厳密には，一生涯雇用を保証するわけではない。日本人の男子平均寿命は70歳代半ばとなったのに，雇用は，各会社の雇用規定により，55歳とか57歳，60歳で打ち切られる。従業員が「定年」(the age for compulsory retirement）に達すると，心身状態や能力にかかわりなく，自動的に職を失う。

Until a decade or so ago, 55 was the universal compulsory retirement age, but corporations have been raising the retirement age gradually. While some have gone as high as 60, those who are sticking to the old age limit still outnumber the others.

The retiring employee receives a lump sum retirement allowance and, with the government pension program, he usually can live without too much financial worry for the rest of his life.

→ **Shūshin-koyõ**

Tenbiki

Because of the **tenbiki** system it is rare for the Japanese corporate employee to receive his full salary each month. In accordance with the law, income tax is withheld at the source, as are payments for health and unemployment insurance and for social security. Under agreement between the company and the labor union, there is also a checkoff for union dues.

Further deductions are arranged through agreement among the company, the employees, and the suppliers of various goods and services. These include installment payments for goods bought through the company, deposits for saving schemes, and premiums for group insurance. Then there are deductions based on company regulations, such as the rental fee for housing provided by the company.

10年くらい前は55歳がふつうの定年年齢だったが，いまは会社側が徐々に引き上げている。だが，年輩者がふえてきたにもかかわらず，古い定年制度を守っている会社も多い。

定年退職者は，一時金で退職手当を支給される。それと国から支給される年金があれば，老後のお金をそれほど心配せずに，どうにかやってゆける。

→終身雇用

天引き

日本の会社員は，「天引き」制度があるので，毎月の給料を額面どおりにまるまる支給されることはない。法律によって，所得税が源泉徴収される。健康保険，失業保険，社会保障などの払込金も差し引かれる。会社と労組との合意により組合費も給料差引きである。

さらに，会社と社員と物品・サービス納入業者との三者取決めで引かれる分がある。会社を通して買った商品の月賦代金，積立貯金，グループ保険の払込金など，まだある。社宅の家賃など，会社の規定にもとづく差引分がある。

Although these different types of **tenbiki** make the monthly pay envelope lighter, it is a convenient system about which employees have few complaints.

Tozama

Tozama is a word which is symbolic of the way Japanese society is constituted. Directly translated, the word means "outside person" or "outsider".

In feudal days, it was customary for people to enter the service of a lord's family when very young and serve for life, or for a son to follow in the footsteps of his father as a retainer to the same lord. Any person who entered the lord's service part-way in his adult life was called a **tozama**.

Today, a person who is hired by a company not straight out of school but after spending some years in another organization is a **tozama**. An **ama-kudari** person is also a **tozama**. In Japan's vertical society, a **tozama** is one who is not "purebred".

→ **Ama-kudari, Chūto-saiyõ, Kogai**

Uogokoro areba mizugokoro

This is a proverb which is used most often in connection with male-female relationships. It means that if one side should display a favorable

こうしたもろもろの「天引き」で，月給袋は軽くなるばかりだが，便利でもあるので，社員から苦情は出ない。

外様

「外様」とは，日本の社会の仕組みを象徴的にあらわすことばである。直訳すると outside person とか outsider となる。

封建時代には，幼少から藩主に仕え，一生同一藩主に仕えるのが当たり前であった。また，その子息も父親の仕える藩主に仕え，父親同様一生同じ藩に属することとなっていた。これが「譜代」の侍であり，一方扶持を離れた浪人が，途中から他家へ仕えたばあいは「外様」と呼ばれた。

今日，学校を出ると同時に入社するのでなく，何年間か他の会社に勤めてから中途入社した者が「外様」といわれている。天下りしてくる人も同様に外様である。日本のタテ社会では，生え抜きでないものは，すべて外様と呼ばれる。

→天下り，中途採用，子飼い

魚心あれば水心

これは男女の間柄をいうときによく使われる諺（proverb）である。本人に憎からず思っている気持ちがあれば，相手

feeling toward the other, the other side would respond in like manner.

A rough translation of the expression would be "if the fish has a heart for the water, the water will have heart for the fish." It expresses like-mindedness or compatibility. In the business world it can be used to show a give-and-take relationship.

English sayings with a similar meaning are: Roll my log and I'll roll yours; Scratch my back and I'll scratch yours; Do as you would be done by.

Yabuhebi

The manager asks his people to make some suggestions on improving his department's operations. Back come a lot of complaints about what he is doing wrong and demands that he mend his ways about certain things. This wasn't what he expected. He has stirred up a hornet's nest, or in Japanese "**yabuhebi ni natta**".

A staff member may make a suggestion which the manager says is excellent and to the proposer's surprise he is assigned to implement the idea which requires a lot of hard extra work. Again, **yabuhebi**.

The word **yabuhebi** translates literally as "snake in the bush" and it means "stirring up the

にもそれに応えようとする気持ちがあることの意。

　ことばどおりに訳すと，"If the fish has the heart for the water, the water will have heart for the fish." 似たような気持ちのあること，とか，気持ちが合致することをいう。商売の世界でいうと，"give‐and‐take"（互いに譲りあう）の関係をいう。

　英語にもこれに似た諺がある。"Roll my log and I'll roll yours." （こっちの丸太をころがしてくれ，そうしたら，そっちの丸太もころがしてやろう）"Scratch my back and I'll scratch yours." （こっちの背中を掻いてくれ，そしたら君の背中も掻いてあげるから）"Do as you would be done by." （君がしてほしいことを人にしてあげなさい）

やぶ蛇

　部長が部の運営の仕方について改善策があれば，なにか提案を出すように，と部下にいう。すると，あそこが悪い，ここがいけないと，たくさん苦情が返ってきた。これこれについては，やり方を変えた方がよい，という要求も出てきた。部長には，思いがけないことだった。"stirred up a hornet's nest"（蜂の巣を突っついた）のである。これを日本語では「やぶ蛇になった」という。

　部下がある提案をする。部長は，そりゃ妙案だとほめて，さっそく実行に移したまえ，と命ずる。驚いたのは部下の方だ。いい出したばかりに，余計な仕事を引っかぶって，あくせく働かねばならぬ羽目となった。これも「やぶ蛇」である。

　やぶ蛇の直訳は "snake in the bush"（やぶの中の蛇）である。"stirring up the snake lying peacefully in the

snake lying peacefully in the bush". So, if you want to say, "Let a sleeping dog lie" or "Don't stir up a hornet's nest", the expression to use in Japanese is **"Sore wa yabuhebi ni narimasu yo"**.

Yakudoshi

One may assume that without a scientific and practical mind, the Japanese would not have been able to reach their present high level of technical and industrial development. As a corollary one might think that such a people would have little use for superstitious beliefs. But no.

Many things in Japanese society are governed by superstitious beliefs. **Yakudoshi** is just one of them. This is the belief that men and women have a predetermined unlucky age when all sorts of misfortune are likely to visit them. During a person's unlucky age, he/she might become extraordinarily cautious and refrain from doing things which ordinarily would be routine.

bush"（やぶの中に静かにしている蛇を突っつき起こした）という意味である。そこで "Let a sleeping dog lie"（眠っている犬を起こすな）とか "Don't stir up a hornet's nest"（蜂の巣をつつくな）の意味のことをいいたいときには，こういえばよい。「それはやぶ蛇になりますよ」

厄年

　日本人が，これほどの素晴らしい技術・産業開発をとげたのは，科学する心，応用する知恵があればこそである。したがって，これほどの成果をあげた国民が，縁起をかつぐ（superstitious belief）なんて，まず誰も思うまい。ところが，さにあらず，なのである。

　日本の社会には，縁起・迷信でことを決めるものがたくさんある。そのひとつが「厄年」。男女を問わず，人間には，もろもろの厄（misfortune）が一度にやってくる不幸な年回りが，前から定められているのだ，という思い込みである。この不幸な年齢になると，その人はとても用心深くなる。ふつうなら，どうということもないのに，手をつけようとしない。

A man's **yakudoshi** is 42 and a woman's 33. Minor unlucky ages in the man's case are 25 and 60. A woman has only one minor unlucky age: 19.

Yoko-meshi

Yoko is lateral or horizontal and **meshi** is meal (lunch or dinner), but if the word is rendered in English as "horizontal meal" it makes no sense. Here, **yoko** is a reference to English or European languages which are written on a horizontal line as opposed to the vertical writing of the Japanese. Thus **yoko-meshi** becomes a business lunch or dinner with visitors from overseas.

Although the Japanese start learning English at the age of 12 in junior high school and continue through senior high school and part of university, they don't seem to make much progress. Thus, eating a meal while conversing in English requires concentration on language, and so they say, "When I have **yoko-meshi** I don't feel as if I had a meal." Perhaps the readers of this book who are not fluent in Japanese may feel that a **tate-meshi** (vertical meal) is similarly something of an ordeal.

Yoroshiku

When parting after a negotiation or a meeting, Japanese businessmen more often than not say "good-bye" with a **yoroshiku** instead of a **sayonara.**

男の大きな厄年は42歳，女は33歳である。小さい厄年は
男25歳と60歳。女の小厄は19歳だけ。

横めし

　字義は，横の食事で，これでは，なんのことかわからな
い。ヨコとは，タテ書きの日本文字にたいする英語など横
書きのことばを意味する。来訪の外人客と一緒にするビジ
ネスランチ，ディナーのことである。

　日本人は中学生以来（12歳）英語を習っているのだが，
どうも語学がうまくない。そのため，英会話をしながらの
食事は考えながらのこととなるから「どうも横めしは食べ
た気がしない」などと，敬遠気味となるわけである。この
本の読者で，日本語の堪能でないあなたが「タテめし」を
食べるのが苦痛であると同様に。

よろしく

　交渉や会議が終わって別れるとき，日本のビジネスマン
は「さようなら」とはいわずに，よく「よろしく」という。
初めて紹介されたとき，初対面のときも，日本人はお互い

When people are introduced or meet for the first time, they also say **yoroshiku** to each other. When a person asks another to convey his best wishes to someone else, he says, "Please say **yoroshiku** to Mr. X".

This versatile word conveys a variety of meanings. In the first case above, it may be "I'm depending on you", "I hope you will take proper action", "Please give it your consideration", "I hope you will give us a favorable reply", etc. Usually the matter in question is not mentioned in concrete terms.

In the second case, it is used in the same way as "How do you do?" or "Pleased to meet you", and carries the nuance of "I hope you will be favorably disposed towards me". In the third case, **yoroshiku** means "Give my best regards to ......" or "Remember me to ......".

Yūkyū-kyūka

This is the term for paid leave. Salaried workers in Japan are given twenty or so paid holidays per year in addition to Sundays, twelve national holidays and, if their company has adopted the 5-day week, Saturdays.

The number of paid holidays depends on the length of service. Generally, it starts with seven

に「よろしく」という。だれかに best wishes を伝える（convey）ように頼むとき「どうかＸさんによろしくいってください」。

なににでもつかえることばだが，意味あいもいろいろある。最初にあげた例は次の意味である。"I'm depending on you."（あなたを頼りにしています）"I hope you will take proper action."（しかるべく措置してくださるものと思っています）"Please give it your consideration."（どうぞ ご配慮のほどを）" I hope you will give us a favorable reply."（色よい返事をお待ちしております）この表現は，問題になっている事柄を具体的に示さないのが普通である。

第2の用例では，"How do you do."（ごきげんいかが）とか "Pleased to meet you."（お会いできてうれしいです）と，つかい方は同じだが，"I hope you will be favorably disposed towards me"（よしなにお計らいくださいますように）というニュアンスがある。第3の用例では，"Give my best regards to ……" とか "Remember me to ……" の意味である。

有給休暇

給料が支払われる休暇（the paid leave）のこと。日本のサラリーマンには，年に20日間くらいの「有給休暇」（paid holidays）がある。もちろん，日曜，祝祭日12日，それに週5日制のところでは土曜も有給の休日に加えられる。

有給休暇の日数は，勤続年数（length of service）による。1年目が年7日，あと年2日ずつふえて，最高20日間といったところだ。

days for the first year and increases by two days each year up to a maximum of twenty.

The older generation, particularly white-collar businessmen, often do not take all the **yūkyū-kyūka** to which they are entitled, because, many say, they are too busy. The younger generation takes paid vacations for granted, and their life-style is influencing the older corporate employees.

It has now become customary for most salaried workers to take a week-long vacation in summer, if they can adjust their work arrangements to make it possible.

→ **Kaki-kyūka**

Zangyō

Zangyō (remain behind to work) is the Japanese word for overtime work. Working overtime is very common in Japanese companies, so much so that workers count upon receiving a certain amount of overtime pay (**zangyō teate**) regularly every month. This is particularly so among factory workers.

Among younger workers, an increasing number prefer more free time than overtime pay which is about 20% more than regular wages.

　年輩の人，とりわけ事務職のビジネスマンは，せっかく有給休暇がありながら，こなそうとしないばあいが多い。忙しくて休んでなんかいられない，というのが口ぐせだ。若い世代になると，有給休暇は当たり前のこととして，がっちり休む。その生活態度に年輩組も感化されるようになってきた。

　いまでは，サラリーマンだと夏に1週間の休暇をとるのはざらである。もっとも，仕事のやりくりをつけて，それだけ休めれば，の話だが。

　→夏期休暇

残業

　「残業」（to remain behind to work）は overtime work のこと。日本の会社では，「残業」はごく当り前のことで，社員は，毎月決まって入る「残業手当」（overtime pay）をあてこんでいる。とくに工場で働く人がそうだ。

　残業手当は，基準賃金より20％以上の割増しだが，それでも若い人は残業よりは働かない方を選ぶ。

Although overtime compensation is not paid to people in managerial positions, generally from section chief level up, they remain behind after working hours more than anybody else — perhaps from a sense often of responsibility or loyalty to the company, or desire to be noticed for promotion, or just for love of work.

→ **Teate**

Zensho shimasu

Zensho shimasu is an expression with an affirmative, positive tone: "I shall do my best to respond to your wishes" or "I shall deal with it accordingly" or "I'll attend to it in a suitable manner" or "I'll fix it up for you". It is a widely used expression in business and life in general.

If you point out to a customer that he hasn't been paying his bills regularly, he will say "**Zensho shimasu**". If you complain that the manufacturer has been sending you substandard goods, he will say "**Zensho shimasu**".

It should be noted that the expression does not commit the speaker to a concrete course of action. It's a general "I'll do my best". Sometimes it happens that you feel relieved by the **zensho shimasu** but the implied action is not taken. The explanation, in such cases, will invariably be "Oh, I tried my best, but ......".

→ **Kangaete okimasu**

ふつう，課長以上の管理職は，残業手当がつかないのに，勤務時間後も残って，だれよりも遅くまで働く。責任感もあろう。会社への忠誠心もあろう。引き立ててもらいたい気持ちもあろう。あるいは，根っからの仕事好きなのかもしれない。

　→手当

善処します

　「善処します」とは「貴意に沿うよう最善を尽くします」（I shall do my best to respond to your wishes) とか「適当に処理します」（I shall deal with it accordingly) とか「しかるべく留意します」（ I'll attend to it in a suitable manner) とか「なんとか取り決めてあげましょう」（I'll fix it up for you) のように肯定的で前向きのニュアンスをこめたことばである。仕事の話でも，日常一般でも，広くつかわれる。

　製造業者から送ってきた品物が規格外れだった。文句をつけると「善処します」。

　ここで注意すべきことは，この表現には，どうこうするという具体的行為をなにも約束していないことである。一般的に「最善を尽くします」というだけである。「善処します」と聞いて，やれ安心と思っても，約束どおりの措置がさっぱりとられていない。どうしたのかと聞く。まず一様に答えが返ってくる。「最善は尽くしたのですが，どうも……」

　→考えておきます

Index:索　　引

216

Japanese Business Glossary
日・本・人・語〈和英対訳〉   定価 880 円

昭和58年 5 月 2 日　第 1 刷発行
昭和59年 8 月25日　第14刷発行

　　　　　　　　　　　　　　　　著者　三菱商事広報室
　　　　　　　　　　　　　　　　発行者　高柳　弘
　発行所　〒103 東京都中央区日本橋本石町 1 の 4　東洋経済新報社
　　　　電話　編集 03(246)5661・販売 03(246)5467　振替 東京3-6518
　　　　本文用紙抄造　三菱製紙　印刷・製本　東洋経済印刷

録音テープ発売のお知らせ

本書には別売カセット・テープが付いております。
本書の特色を効果的に引き出すために，是非ご利用
ください。

● テープ 2 巻セット（C-60，C-90）：定価4,600円　送料240円

———「日・本・人・語」カセット・テープ発売元———

株式会社　金星堂

〒101　東京都千代田区神田神保町3丁目21
TEL：03 (263) 3828 (代)／振替東京4-2636